Style and
Consciousness in
Middle English
Narrative

style and consciousness in middle english narrative

John M. Ganim

Princeton University Press
Princeton, New Jersey

for Alice

Contents

Acknowledgments

I would like to thank the research committee of the University of California, Riverside, for assistance in the preparation of the manuscript and the Humanities Institute for time to pursue my ideas. The library staff, especially the Interlibrary Loan Department, at the University of California, Riverside, was extremely helpful. The editors of *PMLA*, *ELH*, and *The Literary Review* have allowed me to reprint parts of articles that originally appeared in those journals.

I am especially grateful for the teaching, friendship, and scholarship of Alfred David, who inspired and guided the earliest versions of this book. Steven Axelrod and James Dean also read the entire manuscript and made many helpful suggestions. Paul Strohm read some early versions of certain chapters. The resourcefulness and sheer hard work of my research assistant, Linda May, were remarkable. I would also like to thank my editor, Tam Curry. I have plagiarized shamelessly from the brilliant conversation of Linda David. Kathy, Mary Jane, Mike, and especially May Ganim offered practical assistance over the years with their characteristically amused tolerance of the most puzzling member of their family. The list of old friends who have indirectly contributed to the writing of this book would go on and on, but one, Bob Brown, contributed rather more directly to its production. Special thanks, too, to Martin Green, Dan Rubey, Dennis Taylor, Doug Downard, Sam Gosen, and Mark Bernheim. My greatest debt is to Alice Wexler, to whom this book is dedicated.

Style and
Consciousness in
Middle English
Narrative

Introduction

The modern reader who turns to medieval narrative poetry with the expectation of a unified setting and temporal continuity is likely to be disappointed. Indeed, it has become commonplace for recent critics to defend the style and structure of medieval narrative poetry by means of analogy to the visual arts—to a Gothic cathedral, an interlace design, or a panel painting. Yet all narratives must finally respect the limits of time and space. Hence this study proceeds from a number of related assumptions as to the nature of medieval narrative poetry. To the degree that the purpose of any narrative is to tell a story, its plot must somehow unfold in linear time. Since a narrative is perceived as a sequence of episodes, it requires some minimum of linear, temporal continuity. When a narrative is static or discontinuous, its form is to be understood as a variation on a paradigm.[1] Despite the quite different theories of perception, temporality, and the nature of phenomenal reality that were current in the Middle Ages, medieval storytellers had to construct a sequence of logically and temporally connected episodes.

At least in light of philosophy and theology, however, the world in time had always to defer to the world beyond time. Reality derived its meaning not from the connection of particulars in history (or in narrative) but from the influence of the eternal, the otherworldly, the transcendent. The perception of the world by means of sequential and linear understanding was generally held to be an imperfect apprehension of a universal order that could only be appreciated from the perspective of eternity. In order to resolve the quandary in which the limits of time and space place him, the medieval narrative artist must

3

resort to distortion, discontinuity, and a highly conditioned representation of phenomenal reality. The resulting narrative style can tell us a good deal about the poet's attitude towards the nature of life in the earthly realm as well as about the validity of a fiction that takes place in that realm. This is a study of that style.

FOR ALL MY insistence in the following pages on the importance of the temporal dimension in narrative, it is abundantly clear that the poems studied here do not offer the rendering of a realistic time and space continuum that establishes the solidity and verisimilitude of the novel. Despite a recent tendency to stress the fabulous and improbable in the tradition of the novel, the distinction formulated by Ian Watt in *The Rise of the Novel* remains true. The temporal dimension is of less significance in narrative forms before the novel. In classical literature reality can be revealed as a timeless universal. Truth can be unfolded in a moment or a day, as in the temporal and spatial unity of Greek drama. In medieval fictions the manifestations of time "focus attention, not on the temporal flux, but on the supremely timeless fact of death; their role is to overwhelm our awareness of daily life so that we shall be prepared to face eternity." The truths embodied in fiction are always the same, and are equally applicable in different circumstances. There is a consequent lack of interest in "minute-by-minute and day-to-day temporal setting . . . the sequence of events is set in a very abstract continuum of time and space, and allows very little importance to time as a factor in human relationships." Watt's emphasis on the importance of realism in the development of the novel leads to the stress he puts on the concern of Richardson and Fielding with realistic spatial settings. As he points out, "we cannot easily visualize any particular moment of existence without setting it in its spatial context also." Before the development of the novel, narrative space was "unlocalized"; local description, when it was included, was "incidental and fragmentary."[2]

It is true that medieval writers in the end had to defer to the tradition of Boethius and Augustine, a tradition that expressed

4

the profound difference between the temporality of men and the eternity of God. In the most abstract, cerebral way, temporal understanding was regarded as an imperfect, fluctuating faculty. In the most terrible, immediate way, time was regarded as a corrosive force, withering the flesh and rendering futile the pitiful works of men. The expectation of Apocalypse and the contempt for the world did not offer a framework for organizing the works and days of men that might become the subject of narrative fiction, for these versions of history compel us to turn away from the facts of this world. But particularly, though not exclusively, at the end of the Middle Ages, there were available a number of ways of organizing time. Redemption, too, was possible in the fullness of time. In addition, as Augustine tells us, there are ways in which memory offers us a certain liberty from the bondage of time. Augustine himself had a clear grasp of historical notions and exhibited an insistence on continuity and connection in his own writings. From the earliest times, that is, Christian thinkers possessed a grand structure, a world view that provided a cosmological scaffold for the structure of events; yet they also inherited a tradition of careful chronicling, dating, and attending to minutiae from classical antiquity and from the predominantly historical condition of Christianity, that the Incarnation occurred in a real time and place. The impulse was always there to provide logical connections and authenticating details for the events they described. More specifically, an intense historical consciousness seems to have developed from about the twelfth century onwards, what Chenu calls the "new awareness of history" and what Ricardo Quinones calls the "Renaissance discovery of time," a development that clearly had some relationship to the increasing sophistication in narrative forms in that period. The strands of historical thinking that play a substantial part in the culture of the Renaissance are already latent, though not yet fully developed enough to offer a coherent grasp of the structure of events. By the end of the Middle Ages there is no single "medieval sense of time." There exists, rather, a complex and often contradictory availability of different systems to organize events, though admittedly these rarely cohere in any usable synthesis.[3]

Contemporary criticism has emphasized the sophistication of medieval literature and with good reason rejects the condescension of earlier critics towards what was regarded as naive, fumbling, or primitive. Yet there is a hesitant tone in even the best medieval poetry. One way of explaining it is to argue for a prevalence of irony rather than a lack of art. But in a literature influenced by the most searching questions of Christian doctrine, that irony is at least as much directed against the self-containment of the work of art as it is against the action of this or that character or episode. Even language and rhetoric, however much they may struggle against such limitations, are bound by the very limits of time and space that circumscribe our imperfect human imagination. What we see as a unique form is not only a different aesthetic from ours or a symbolic structure that asks to be read in a nonmimetic fashion; it is also a way of perceiving and organizing experience. That the novel requires a mastery and consciousness of space and time as continuous and causal phenomena does not necessarily mean that the novel is a higher form of development. Yet it is difficult not to think of those predecessors as antecedents, and it is well to keep in mind Bishop Hurd's perceptive, if sentimental, notion of Gothic form:

> The Gothic method of design in poetry may be, in some sort, illustrated by what is called the Gothic method of design in gardening. A wood or grove cut out into many separate avenues or glades was among the most favourite of the works of art, which our fathers attempted in this species of cultivation. These walks were distinct from each other, had each, their several destination, and terminated on their own proper objects. Yet the whole was brought together and considered under one view, by the relation which these various openings had, not to each other, but to their common and concurrent center.[4]

Hurd follows this "Gothic method of design" into the province of poetry. Indeed, it seems as if the defense of medieval narrative forms must rest on the shaky ground of this analogy, for most modern critics who would alert us to the different nature of medieval narrative make their case by reference to medieval visual arts. The validity of such analogies is one of the recurrent debates in literary criticism, but I want to argue here that the questions involved acquire a special importance in the case of medieval narrative.

A BROADLY CULTURAL point of view, which is in no way naive, might not consider medieval narrative problematic. After all, if a Gothic cathedral could yoke together its diverse elements, if panels and sculptures could tell stories by means of isolated scenes, if painting tended towards abstraction and pattern rather than representation and perspective, why should we expect medieval narrative poetry to present a clearly subordinated sequence of events? For an answer to this question I am indebted to a theoretical discussion that takes as its starting point Lessing's *Laocoön*.[5] There, of course, Lessing sets out to establish the limits of poetry and of the other arts. Poetry is made up of signs or sounds that are to be understood in sequence, and therefore the proper subject of poetry is the representation of events that take place in time. The plastic arts are made up of juxtaposed forms and colors that are perceived at once. Therefore, the proper subject of the plastic arts is the representation of bodies in space. No one would quibble with Lessing's formulations. In fact, they seem almost commonplace today. But it is equally obvious that at certain times art forms tend to strain against their limits and occasionally transcend them. The roles become reversed. Art seeks to portray subjects of movement and time; literature asks to be perceived in a nonconsecutive manner. A number of modern, and medieval, examples spring to mind.

Under the aegis of Gide's remark that Lessing's *Laocoön* is one of those books that it is good to affirm or refute every twenty or thirty years, Joseph Frank, in a compelling essay, makes the case for "Spatial Form in Modern Literature."[6] The form of modern poetry depends on the reader's connection of separate words, phrases, and sentences. Instead of following the time-logic of language, modern poetry adopts the space-logic of the visual arts. Instead of the sequential development of a theme, meaning is generated by the juxtaposition of images. Hence we have to perceive the whole structure of the poem before individual elements make sense. Cross-references become more important than development. We are asked to read a poem as if it were a sculpture, reacting to its various parts simultaneously. In the modern novel there is a similar spatialization of time. Instead of a sequential narrative, "attention is fixed on the interplay of relationships within the immobilized time-area" (p. 15). The novel, too, aspires to the condition of the modern poem, with a space-logic rather than a time-logic, a structure of juxtaposition rather than of sequence.

The reason I have described Frank's theory here in some detail is that critics have thought about applying the idea of "spatial form" to medieval narrative. To Eugene Vinaver medieval narrative is like "the flowering of this same form within our modern 'poetic space' from James Joyce to T. S. Eliot, from Proust to Valéry, and beyond."[7] Morton Bloomfield, however, asserts, "Time is of the essence of narrative, which is, as Lessing long ago pointed out, sequential, but narrative writers all more or less try to transcend this limitation without at the same time destroying completely the temporality of narrative. Samuel Johnson speaks of diversifying narrative by 'retrospection and anticipation.' Chaucer knew this secret as all his narratives show." And in a footnote Bloomfield criticizes Frank's essay on spatial form because "the 'neutralization' of time is not only a modern phenomenon. It might also be argued that all art strains against its limitations of form."[8]

On a more elementary level, of course, there is a certain degree to which spatial and temporal indications are inseparable from the most basic facts of plot. What happens between the acts of a play? If the playwright wishes to suggest, say, the passing of time or the change of scene, he may just tell us, by stage directions, by makeup, by the simple appearance of another set of characters. Characters may change, age, or die. Or in a play that observes strict unity, time passes before us. The plot unfolds continuously. In any case, the audience can usually decide for itself. The stage is a continuous frame. The audience is the observer of a presented reality and can put the pieces together. This is not ordinarily the case in an extended narrative fiction.[9] Instead, the imaginative configuration is being represented rather than being acted before our eyes. Hence we are more dependent on the storyteller's hints and outright statements about the transitions between scenes. On the most obvious level of storytelling, transitions are crucial. How does Odysseus travel from one adventure to the next? How does Beowulf come to Heorot? Even if the world is one of fantasy, we must have signposts through wonderland. And in allegorical narrative the transitions between loci and the intervals of time may have semantic significance. Thus at the simplest level of storytelling, transitions provide a basic, literal sense of the order between scenes. "Meanwhile, back at the ranch . . . ," and we are oriented in time and space. Even critics who would alert us to the fact that some medieval narratives seem to disregard logical and temporal sequence would admit that "the 'flow of events' is never entirely excluded . . . from any known epic poem."[10] Perhaps an audience used to the exigencies of oral performance would worry less about certain omissions. Yet every poet had to be concerned to some extent with building a scene for his action, "just as dramatic performances demand a stage set, however primitive."[11] Thus no matter what other meaning we allow the contortions of medieval narrative, its study requires attention to the purely functional qualities of temporal and spatial elements.

From a broader point of view, the pattern of indicators of time and space in a given work (or a genre) can shape a significant structure of its own. Some of these structures are self-evident: heaven, hell, and middle earth in the geography of the mystery cycles; the alternation of almost primitive conceptions of sacred and profane spaces in *Beowulf*; the endless sequence of bower and castle and wood in the chivalric romances. Such a structuring of space indicates to the audience the work's conception of its own importance and stature as well as its vision of the world. But there is also a unique quality to the way in which the individual poet adapts these basically generic conceptions of the world to the circumstances of his narrative. The artful playing upon that expectation lifts a poem above its generic siblings and reveals in subtle ways the identification or tension between artist and audience that is one of my primary interests here. The very evidences of phenomenal reality, the dimensions of time and space, in fiction, and particularly medieval fiction, are not only referents to the world we see but are signs in themselves that derive their power less from fidelity to our observation than from their own system of construction, proportion, relation, and reversal. This is why the analogy to Gothic architecture is both so helpful and so limiting, because it helps us to see that there is a formal pattern at the same time that it forces us to "read" the pattern as we would that of a painting; we also need, however, to stress the dimensions of temporality that might qualify that pattern and that generate meaning in narrative.

The style of many medieval narratives, then, is a way of allowing that art has limits, and it does so by laying bare those limits. The unity that the realistic novel offers to a later audience is a unity derived from a faith in the causality of events, economic conditions, history and biography, all of which can create destinies in fiction as they do in life. In the medieval view such conditions unaided can create only the inexorable cycle of fortune. Thus medieval narrative poems often seem to require an imposed unity, a structure or pattern external to the material at hand. Their style admits that such unity cannot be obtained from the imitation of the phenomenal world alone. Such poetry is not only limited by the vicissitudes of time and space, it admits that our time and space are themselves limited.

I have read the various discontinuities, gaps, juxtapositions, and fragmentary transitions of medieval narrative as significant forms in themselves, comments on the action, and distancing devices. Transitions that we might expect to operate as conduits instead function as hinges in the action. The reader is forced to correlate the scale of various scenes, since the transitions do not adequately subordinate them. The effort at making such connections on the part of readers is a distancing factor, forcing them to reconsider the action. The audience is invited into the world of the poem and allowed to recreate the action in their imaginations, but only at times, only with reservations, only with the reminder that the contemplation or imitation of the phenomenal world is not enough.

NONE OF THESE questions, from the most specific to the most general, can be considered in isolation from the circumstances of the reception of medieval texts. The artist was not a free agent and his work was not an independent, self-justifying entity. "Whereas a man may have noon audience, / Nought helpeth it to tellen his sentence," says Chaucer's Host. The awareness of the poet's responsibility to his audience is everywhere both implicit and explicit. Medieval poetics never lost sight of Horace's dictum, that the function of poetry was to delight and to teach, and if delight and pleasure were suspect goals, they could always be rationalized by the latter aim. From both its classical and patristic authorities, as these were understood in the late Middle Ages, medieval literary theory emphasized the essentially rhetorical nature of poetry.[12] Both poetry and theory owed their allegiance less to aesthetic unity than to the effect of art upon the audience. The notions of creative individuality and originality are nascent, but the dominant ideal of literary creation is that truth is already imbedded in a more or less fixed moral order and that the responsibility of the poet is to reveal that order. This enterprise becomes increasingly difficult in the late Middle Ages. The purity of such a goal, adequate in many respects to didactic and sacred poetry, is in many more respects compromised by a literature that creates fictions of the secular world. At least part of this difficulty derives from the contradiction of imaging truths that exist beyond time within nar-

11

ratives that center increasingly on the sophisticated represen-
tation of mundane and fleeting experience. The management
of this contradiction remains a constant, if implicit, concern in
much late medieval narrative. The argument of this study is
that from this anxiety derive the best and most characteristic
features of late medieval narrative. Within every work there is
a system of checks and balances that suggests the possible range
of responses. This is true of modern as well as medieval works.
But it is a necessary corollary of medieval fiction that such
systems acquire an essential importance.

For an approach that locates these large concerns in the details
of style and the movement of a particular text, I have been
guided by the work of Erich Auerbach. I have borrowed from
his *Mimesis* the procedure of closely examining specific passages
and then moving to larger cultural themes implied by the style
of that text.[13] My description of the relation of poet and audience
follows Auerbach's analysis of Dante's style in *Literary Lan-
guage and Its Public in Late Antiquity and the Middle Ages*.
In most vernacular literature, Auerbach observes, the address
of the narrator is nearly always to the listener rather than to
the reader, and furthermore, its purpose is to gain the sympathy
and attention of the audience. But a properly Christian style
interweaves "accusation and self-accusation, earnestness and
humility, the superiority of the teacher and brotherly love. The
dialectical and Augustinian urgency in the relationship between
author and audience . . . is infrequent and nowhere highly
developed in vernacular writing before Dante."[14] One of my
themes in the following chapters is the highly qualified devel-
opment of this "dialectical urgency" in Middle English narrative
poetry. Although Auerbach's relatively restricted description of
"figura" in his famous essay of that name has been broadly
applied in medieval studies, in the criticism of English medieval
literature at least, his more promising methodology, a version
of cultural stylistics, has been less widely employed. Yet it seems
to me to be the most valuable avenue to those dimensions of
medieval texts that remain intractable to other sorts of criticism,
what Peter Dronke calls "a poet's concern with unconfined

12

meaning as against fixed signification, with the evocative and enigmatic as against the sphere of fixed correspondences."[15]

THE FOLLOWING CHAPTERS describe these concerns in texts chosen from the thirteenth, fourteenth, and fifteenth centuries. Chapter 1 discusses two of the earlier Middle English romances, *Havelok the Dane* and *King Horn*. These romances have usually suffered by comparison with twelfth-century French chivalric romances. In this chapter I seek to locate in these English romances a characteristic voice, one that is of some importance both in its own right and also as a context for the great productions of fourteenth-century English literature. Twelfth-century French romance concerned itself with the examination of ideal aristocratic values and explored the contradictions inherent in those values. Moreover, a certain "professional" distance between poet and audience is ascertainable in those texts. But in the early English romances there is an assumption of community between narrator and audience. We may be conscious that the social order established at the end of their stories is fragile enough, but we have no doubt that history, and the poet, are on our side. Paradoxically, the assertion of community results in a problematic series of shifts in tone, in contrast, for example, to the perfectly adjusted tone of Chrétien's romances. The early Middle English romances aspire to the rhetorical situation of epic without facing some of the larger questions raised by epic. In fact, throughout, these romances anxiously pass over certain questions, almost consciously avoid certain paths of development that might radically challenge the values of their audience.

We are drawn into the experience of the characters far more often and deeply in the most significant fourteenth-century narratives. That is part of what we mean when we speak of the "sophistication" of poems such as *Sir Gawain and the Green Knight* and Chaucer's *Troilus and Criseyde* (one might similarly include an earlier fourteenth-century poem such as *Sir Orfeo*, which I do not discuss here). The schematic quality of a romance like *King Horn* works like a score, referring us to a common

13

physical and emotional reality, but in no way recreating that reality, perhaps because the complexity of that experience would compromise the meaning of the work, whereas in the four-teenth-century texts I discuss, such experience creates the mean-ing of the work. In these later texts the reader's values, even our perception and understanding, are displayed as relative, partial, imperfect. The limits of narrative, a matter of skill in some earlier romances, here become a matter of meaning. And it is in this group of poems, written within a fairly limited time period, that the dialectical potential of a Christian poetic is ful-filled within secular narrative poems. It is, however, a strained and negative balance, which could hardly fuel a tradition.

Chapter 2 describes the relatively subtle process of disorien-tation of our expectations in *Sir Gawain and the Green Knight*. The structural order of the poem, which has been pointed out in some important studies, is in fact partly subverted by its stylistic techniques. In *Troilus and Criseyde*, the subject of chap-ter 3, Chaucer first suggests and then undercuts a series of poses that the audience is made to take towards the action. We are made aware of our own need to impose a temporal fiction upon a world resistant to such order; indeed, linear logic and lan-guage, the very stuff of the poem itself, are called into question by our implication in its processes. In the fifteenth century a didactic, fixed relation replaces this dialectic. The poetry seems to assume that the reader requires a system of moral buttresses. The great achievement of the fourteenth-century poets, their mastery of irony, is bypassed. Chapter 4 illustrates this change with the poetry of Lydgate. Finally, in chapter 5 I read Hen-ryson's *Testament of Cresseid* as an antidote to the excess of fifteenth-century poetry, through a concentration that limits the range of our response.

In the simplest terms, then, what this study offers is a de-scription of the ways in which the medieval narrative poet struc-tures a world for his audience, what M. M. Bakhtin would call the "chronotope" of late Middle English narrative.[16] The di-mensions of that world are created explicitly and implicitly by the nuances of his style and the shape of his narrative. Addresses to the reader, cues as to how to interpret the plot or the motivation of various characters, even critical commentary included by the narrator have been regarded here not as dispensable asides, but as essential elements. Those passages that connect sequences in time and space and which have been slighted as evidence either for a lack of interest in horizontal unity or for a primitive sense of artistic construction are here regarded as crucial units that signal our skepticism, complicity, or belief in the independent existence of the fiction before us. I have tried to determine what the attitude of poet and audience was towards the validity of a story that clearly took place in the earthly world, what adjustments the poet made in the representation of that world because of this attitude, and what sorts of narrative organization the poet imposed on events and objects that were regarded as largely amenable only to chaos, transience, and apocalypse.

CHAPTER 1

Community and Consciousness in Early Middle English Romance

a number of scholars have described the change in society, sensibility, and form that surrounded the transformation of epic into romance.[1] Most studies, however, have concerned themselves with the elegant Old French productions of the twelfth century or have debated the degree of overlap and continuity between the two genres. The shift from heroic to chivalric values, from social struggle to individual quest, from concern with the survival of the entire community to concern with the perfection of specific class ideals, all these have been documented and explained. The road that takes us from the gloom of *Beowulf* to the glitter of Chrétien's romances crosses barriers of language, social structure, taste, and historical change, but it is a road that has been mapped in some detail.

One reason why the early Middle English romances have not as often been taken seriously is that in most respects they seem to represent a decline in literary history:

> *Beowulf* was composed for persons of quality, *Havelok* for the common people. Old English narrative poetry was, in its day, the best obtainable; English metrical romances were known by the authors, vendors and consumers of them to be inferior to the best, i.e. to the French; and, consequently, there is a rustic, uncourtly air about them. Their demeanour is often lumbering, and they are sometimes conscious of it.[2]

I do think that the poets were often "conscious of it," even to the point of playing with an occasional sophisticated air and

16

sometimes contrasting a rapid and deftly constructed narrative with details and phrases that, though they were perhaps striking, were also rustic and quaint. This is not to argue that the *Havelok*-poet was nearly as sophisticated as Chaucer in such a respect. But he thought he knew what he was good for, and he liked to show it.

From a broader point of view, this note of rusticity, even of naiveté, has a certain rhetorical function, and it is this function that I want to explain here. These romances announce potentially epic themes and then retreat from the implications of those themes. They seem to manifest a sense of history, growth, and change and suddenly retreat into a timeless utopian vision of existence. They sometimes represent the dimensions of physical and social reality in profoundly disturbing detail and then counter that sense of reality with comic or grotesque devices. The conceptions of time and space implicit in the narrative structure of these romances differ from such conceptions in either chivalric romance or in epic. They borrow the conventions of courtly romance but use those conventions to appeal to the reader in a radically different way.

There is no question that French courtly romance was the most characteristic genre of high medieval culture, in much the same way that Gothic architecture was the dominant architectural mode. But in twelfth-century France, romance had flourished in a rarefied atmosphere, that of court patronage, with an elite audience capable of comprehending an often esoteric code of social values. Indeed, the very source of courtly literature is in its insistence that its audience is exceptional and could understand things that a larger audience could not.[3] It was an art of delicate balance—on the one hand, hints and cues that serve as signs to the initiated; on the other, long and sometimes tiresome exploration of states of consciousness, fused in an action of fantastic adventure. In a totally different social and literary situation, that of thirteenth-century England, in which class distinctions, though clear, seemed to require less elaborate markings and in which, in comparison, the flowering of provincial courts had never advanced that far, this art was under

17

strains that threatened to transform it beyond recognition. This is not merely to repeat the observation that English romances are less refined and therefore more popular than their French antecedents. Rather it is to describe an entirely different literary and rhetorical situation. Far from confirming the elite nature of a court audience, early Middle English romance speaks to a larger community, and the narrating voice makes an attempt to include itself and its audience in that world. The "flaws" that result are only contradictions if we abide by whatever generic standards we draw from French romance. The result is a form in Middle English romance that borrows widely from many different genres in an attempt to establish its own authenticity and that moves towards a form less courtly and exclusive and more encyclopedic and inclusive, a combination that has considerable implications for the development of later Middle English poetry.

Not only does English romance borrow from a wide variety of genres, which in themselves each imply a specific audience, but it borrows from a wide spectrum of romances.[4] During the high point of Middle English romance, romance as a genre in France was already two hundred years old, and without too much exaggeration one could point not only to clearly aristocratic but also to popular romances, as well as to those that combined such elements. Often the earliest English romances have the quality of anthologies; consistency of tone is one of their problems. Elements that derive from lyric or epic, from delicate *lai*, from *chanson de geste*, from chivalric romance, are found together, as if jerked from their original historical context. But this problematic situation also leads to Middle English literature's greatest strengths—the multiplicity of perspective and wide appeal of such works as *The Canterbury Tales*—as well as to a kind of included criticism of an entire tradition that I, along with other critics, believe is found in *Sir Gawain and the Green Knight*.

As I argued in my Introduction, this inclusive but contradictory attitude towards the action is most clearly evidenced in those passages that create the sense of time and space in the poem. Hence the following description of *Havelok the Dane*, the most interesting of these early Middle English romances, concentrates on such transitional scenes. After some conclusions about the effect of these scenes I move to a discussion of *King Horn* in light of these conclusions, and then to an attempt to characterize the mentality of the early Middle English romances.

Havelok the Dane is based on a nicely merged dual plot. The king of Denmark dies, leaving his heir, Havelok, in the hands of one Earl Godard. Godard, not about to give up such power, imprisons the boy and his two sisters. He slits the throats of the two girls but spares the prince, ordering a fisherman, Grim, to drown the boy. Meanwhile, we are told of a similar situation in England, where a king has died, leaving his daughter, Goldboro, in the hands of an equally nefarious guardian, one Godrich. Godrich, who dislikes the idea of handing the country over to a mere girl, locks her up in a tower, and prevents her marriage to anyone save the strongest man in England in ironic loyalty to the oath he has sworn to her father. We return to the story of Havelok. Grim, converted by a magic flame that comes out of the hero's mouth, has spared the child, adopted him, and migrated to England. In time of want Havelok travels to Lincoln, where he works as a cook's helper, engages in sports, and establishes a reputation as the strongest man in England. Godrich, delighted that he can break Goldboro's claim to the throne by marrying her to such a commoner, forces the match. The marriage presumably lacks spark, until she too sees a magic flame shoot from the mouth of her husband, notes a magic birthmark, and recognizes by these signs his royal origins. At any rate, Havelok grows conscious of his position, gathers an army, which becomes larger and larger, overthrows both Godrich and Godard, unites England and Denmark, and settles down with Goldboro and their fifteen children, who all become kings and queens, to a long and happy reign. The action takes place in slightly over three thousand lines, which assumes a somewhat more leisurely pace than most early Middle English romances.

19

Whenever the narrator of *Havelok* shifts the scene of his action, he feels compelled to impress upon us the importance and seriousness of his theme, either through an elevation of style or through outright statement. His perspective is suddenly enlarged, and he comprehends units as large as miles and years:

> Fro londe woren he bote a mile—
> Ne were it neuere but ane hwile—
> That it ne bigan a wind to rise
> Out of the north—men calleth "bise"—
> And drof hem intil Engelond,
> That al was sithen in his hond—
> His, that Hauelok was the name—
> But or, he hauede michel shame,
> Michel sorwe, and michel tene,
> And yete he gat it al bidene;
> Als ye shulen nou forthward lere,
> Yf that ye wilen therto here.
>   In Humber Grim bigan to lende,
> In Lindeseye, rith at the north ende.
> Ther sat is ship upon the sond. . . .
>   (721-735)[5]

This passage is a good starting point for a study of how the poet constructs and uses the "world"—the time, space, and scene—of his fiction and also of the anxiety the poet feels towards the attitude of his audience to this world, for at the same time that he exerts this effort to shift the locus of his action, he also reminds us that this story is about serious issues, which make a claim to be read as history.

In these few lines the narrator seems especially concerned with establishing a sense of place. He tells us exactly where the ship has gone. The fateful "bise" is more than an accident, for it takes Havelok to the proper place at the proper time, a providence the poet calls to our attention. Yet his geography is schematic. This world is like a map, neither felt nor experienced, nor is it described in the easy and proficient style of the poet's most vibrant local scenes. He provides enough information here to avoid the sense of scene thrown against scene, but at best, the world between remains abstract, though with the convincing accuracy of an annal. More necessary to his narrative, especially a narrative about heroes and heroines growing up, with a theme of succession and a plot device of coincidence, is the establishment of time referents. Within the fairly limited compass of a hundred lines surrounding the passage quoted above, we are given three significant time indications. One deals with plot time, one with the narrator's and audience's sense of duration, and one with historical time. The last lines I have quoted above (728-732) return us abruptly and gravely to the time of the narrator and his audience, hence emphasizing the importance of this journey as a turning point in the narrative. However, we can also feel a qualified note in such narrative self-importance, which tells us a good deal about the relationship of poet to audience, as expressed in the somewhat apologetic line: "Yf that ye wilen therto here." Such humbleness comes, of course, precisely at the moment when the pieces of the narrative seem at their farthest point apart, yet also at the point when they are about to come together, and both author and audience know this. The shift to historical time is contained in those lines that have always attracted critics who praise *Havelok*'s realism:

> And for that Grim that place aute,
> The stede of Grim the name laute;
> So that Grimesbi calleth alle
> That theroffe speken alle;
> And so shulen men callen it ay,
> Bituene this and domesday.
>
> (743-748)

I do not think that these lines mean the poet of *Havelok* is a thirteenth-century precursor of local color and regional writing. First, the narrator's elevated perspective seems to work against an entirely local flavor. Second, the passage is part of the entirely conventional time indication, in this case putting all of us— characters, narrator, auditors, and Grimsby itself—into the framework of historical time. The narrator wants to emphasize the drama and importance of this journey for the plot. The brief reference to apocalyptic history is another distancing factor. It puts the story into a larger reality, just as the first time indicator "woke" us up from the fiction itself. Yet this epic appeal is suddenly reduced in the next few lines by the humble and local place names, which neither demand nor display such grandeur. Finally, the plot time indicator tells us that while all these distancing factors have taken up our attention, twelve years have passed, during which, while we have been floating around in history and rhetoric, Grim has been working:

> Thusgate Grim him fayre ledde:
> Him and his genge wel he fedde
> Wel twelf winter other more:
> Hauelok was war that Grim swank sore
> For his mete, and he lay at hom:
> He thouthe, "Ich am nou no grom. . . ."
> (785-790)

And while Grim has been working, Havelok has grown up. It is an important fact, though thrown out at us indirectly. The passage of those twelve years is not at all indicated to us by the wonderful scenes of Havelok eating and Grim fishing. They are indeed splendid scenes in their own right. But they are static and separable rather than dynamic parts of the narrative. The poet has to provide essential narrative information in scenes other than those in which he describes the most distinctive actions of his characters.

The smaller transitions are handled more deftly. An excellent example of the proficiency of the poet in these smaller units is the scene in which Havelok leaves Grim to go out on his own. Starving, barefoot, unemployed, it is his social nadir, the king as lumpenproletarian:

> He tok the sheres of the nayl,
> And made him a couel of the sayl,
> And Hauelok dide it sone on.
> Hauede he neyther hosen ne shon,

> Ne none kines other wede;
> To Lincolne barfot he yede.
> Hwan he kam ther, he was ful wil:
> Ne hauede he no frend to gangen til;
> Two dayes ther fastinde he yede,
> That non for his werk wolde him fede;
> The thridde day herde he calle:
> "Bermen, bermen, hider forth alle!"
> Poure that on fote yede
> Sprongen forth so sparke of glede.
> Hauelok shof dune nyne or ten
> Rith amidewarde the fen,
> And stirte forth to the kok,
> Ther the erles mete he tok
> That he bouthe at the brigge:
> The bermen let he alle ligge,
> And bar the mete to the castel,
> And gat him there a ferthing wastel.
>   (857-878)

There is, I think, no need to emphasize the Christic paradigm of Havelok's ordeal. We could search through a thousand literatures and always find a heroic ordeal similar to Havelok's. As Auerbach has shown, Christianity, and the specifically devotional intensity of this period, allowed the mixture of the humblest details with the highest spiritual and literary aspirations.[6] All I would maintain at this point, however, is that the first half of this passage is clearly of a mythic dimension.

Our interest is in the way in which this passage, clearly a transition from Grimsby—on the road to Lincoln, to the town, over the Witham bridge, and on to the castle—organizes the space of the narrative for us. When Grim and his family migrated from Denmark, the journey was narrated in an almost epic conventional voice, from a distance, in a way that involved a good deal of strain on the poet's style. The shorter movement of Havelok to Lincoln in the first half of this passage is handled with a good deal more confidence, though it is an aspect of the

23

mythic dimension of the story: the deposed king, barefoot, starving, alone, clad in the sail which Grim takes from his ship. He fasts for two days and is saved by a voice on the third, a time period that owes less allegiance to narrative realism than to mythic resonance. Suddenly, in a stylistic moment that reminds us of Langland, we are brought down to earth with a markedly earthly and unmistakably naturalistic cry: "Bermen, bermen, hider forth alle!" And we are in a world, and a specific street, filled with a social reality of great and almost poignant detail. That the cook who calls for help should be so rushed suggests the quite awful reality of famine, in an image that would not be all that exotic in some parts of the world today. And as Havelok bowls down his fellow workers, we wonder what happened to the aura of Christian humility that surrounded his journey to Lincoln.

The mythic sobriety of his journey in the first few lines of this passage disappears. The spatial organization of the second half is specific and moves us quickly along from city to bridge to castle. The tempo reflects Havelok's own energy, I suppose, his willingness to work, and the fact that his fortune has changed. In addition, we now know that the larger theme of union with Goldboro and revenge upon their usurpers has some realistic basis since Havelok is in the employ of Godard and has access to him. The bustle of the street is suggested but not described in detail. The careful "three days" of Havelok's starvation was mythic and otherworldly. But the carelessly accounted nine or ten battered porters are paradoxically more likely to convince us of the "reality" of the scene. Havelok, carrying the food to the castle, becomes more tangible then the figure who "To Lincolne barfot . . . yede." The movement to the castle is more comprehensible and more able to suggest literal life than Havelok's outlined journey to Lincoln.

Whenever the poem shifts its locus of action, it cannot help also shifting the social as well as the geographic surroundings. In fact, it tends to see geography and scenery almost in class terms. The fishing village, the town, the castle, correspond to different levels of society, of modes of life. But there is a limit to *Havelok*'s realism. True, we can learn a great deal about the poem's social milieu from the fact that the porters run so quickly to the cook and from the fact that it is the cook who is the contact between castle and town. However, such serious, problematic realism is quickly dispelled by the poet: "Alle made he dem dun falle." The poet defends himself, and perhaps his audience, from the texture of quite real social conflict behind all these entertaining details by a sort of zany cartoon hyperbole. It is classic depression comedy. Such caricature also distends our perception of a "realistic" street scene, confusing our spatial orientation, as if the poet were putting off the possibility of too many questions about the mimetic, social, and even moral intent of the story.

This pattern, we might note, is repeated throughout the poem: a static, almost epic background, suddenly filled with a remarkable sense of life, realism, local immediacy, then, before we can question the contradiction between these two stylistic tendencies, a comic synthesis of the two into a cartoonlike hyperbolic distortion. The same stylistic pattern and the same identification of geography with social class is found in the transition that takes Havelok and his new bride Goldboro back to the town of Grimsby. Havelok decides that the threat to his own life and the possibility that "men sholde don his leman shame" are too great in Lincoln:

> Forthi he token another red:
> That thei sholden thenne fle
> Til Grim, and til hise sones thre;
> Ther wenden he altherbest to spede,
> Hem forto clothe and for to fede.
> The lond he token under fote—
> Ne wisten he non other bote—
> And helden ay the rithe sti
> Til he komen to Grimesby.
> Thanne he komen there, thanne was Grim ded . . .
> (1194-1203)

25

Havelok discovers when he gets to Grimsby that Grim has died, but his children are still alive and they offer themselves and their possessions to the couple. We note again that the poet seems incapable of changing his scene without letting the facts of life intrude: "Hem forto clothe and for to fede." The locales have names, Lincoln and Grimsby, but the movement of the couple is recounted by means of the more economical carto-graphic perspective of the narrator.

That cartographic perspective also conditions the realism of the journey. Havelok and his wife move in the same mythical way that Havelok, barefoot and alone, came to Lincoln. We wonder in fact,what the "rithe [sti]" is. The line is unfortunately mangled. What does the direction indicate? To the right? The most direct route? A moral quality? It could easily be a desperate rhyme. But why had Havelok not heard until now of Grim's death? How long has Grim been dead? And by extension, how long has Havelok been in Lincoln? On the one hand, these may be naive questions that we are not supposed to ask, but on the other hand, the poem does offer half answers. The poet is again straining his style, heightening it, in order to rearrange his characters into dramatic confrontations in which everyone— Havelok, Grim's family, Goldboro, the Angel—has set speeches. So perhaps all the spatial indications we need are stage direc-tions. But the very ambiguity or absence of those indications and the fact that this transition hinges together two quite dif-ferent scenes is also indicative of some larger patterns.[7]

In Lincoln we had a marriage, political plans, ambitions, class "conflicts," fear, a city. In Grimsby we have a group of loyal retainers, dreams, magic conversions, comfort, and despite the lower social standing of the inhabitants, a sense that they all recognize and respect "the right way," the natural order. Even the gap between rich lords and starving porters in Lincoln is resolved here in favor of a "middle" class, for Grim's sons, *nouveau riche* fish entrepreneurs, have done well for them-selves. And significantly, it is in Grimsby that the political and social contradictions that arose in Lincoln—that Goldboro must marry a commoner, that the couple would starve, that their marriage would be uneasy—are all resolved by ordination, as if by magic. The road from Lincoln to Grimsby is not only a physical road.

Everyday life, though it bursts from every scene, is only uneasily integrated into the narrative. I have examined above, with a close eye to formal and narrative elements, the passage in which Havelok, under Grim's care, migrates to England. In that passage the poet was working with fairly conventional narrative elements, straining to achieve a flexibility and fluidity for which his style and immediate literary models are at this point historically unprepared. If we read the passage only with an eye to content, however, its variety of realistic themes is extraordinary. Within the compass of a few hundred lines we travel through social classes from kings to commoners, through economic periods from plenty to starvation, and in however stylized a way, we worry about politics, weather, food, clothing, travel directions, and business. So to some extent *Havelok the Dane* does demand for itself a special niche in the classification of romance, rebelling both against the strict class interest of romance and against its stylized and formal unreality. It might well belong to what we have come as common readers to consider a peculiarly "English" strain of literature, filled with God's plenty, genre scenes, robust and hearty details, looking life straight in the eye. But it must also be pointed out that the style of the narrative prevents this realism from crucially influencing the action of *Havelok*. All this life is recorded, to be sure, but it remains supplementary. The beginning and the end of *Havelok* sound very much like a verse chronicle.[8] The natural ground of *Havelok the Dane*, as we learn from both the introductory and concluding passages, is one of peace, order, and fecundity, and that which disturbs that peace is not only evil but unnatural and should be punished in kind. When Godrich is executed, when Havelok punishes his attackers, we can forget both balance and compassion. We are certain, with the poet and his audience, that such retribution is indeed the wrath of God and his earthly king, as we indeed know that any absorption in

27

such nihilism and violence is a fairly safe business, for eventually we will return to a natural ground of stability.

Significantly, the poet uses a narrative style in both the opening passage, describing the life and death of the old kings, and in the concluding passage, describing the return of the kingdom to Havelok, which is very much like the style of an aristocratic chronicle. For all the mixing of classes in the poem, the normal state of things, in both the beginning and the end of the poem, is communicated in a style that suggests a rigid class order.

We are meant to compare the death of Aethelwold, dignified and peaceful, with that of Godrich, outrageous and unnatural. The lesson is that a man dies as he lives. Aethelwold, and a number of other good characters, are described time and again as the best that ever rode a horse. Godrich and Godard, however, at their death, also end up riding horses, though backwards, and face down, with their noses in the horses' "crich," an almost Dantesque suitability of punishment. But the contrast between good and evil characters goes further than that. We are told that except for his soul Aethelwold's greatest concern at his death is for the safety of his daughter. Godrich and Godard, on the other hand, are punished precisely because of the way in which they treat their charges. In the abstract, of course, their crime is usurpation, disloyalty, and treason to one's knightly oath. In the concrete, however, their villainy is communicated to us by the way in which they treat their charges, the children they have sworn to protect. It becomes a battle, not so much of political forces and dynasties, but of generations. In many romances we find such alignments between the hero and his disenfranchised followers against usurpers. Odysseus, disguised as a beggar, had to fight them in the form of his wife's suitors. Havelok, a peasant, fights against Godrich, who, we learn, is a propounder of a new order in law. Romance as a mode frequently pits the traditionalists and the young against the new men.

Towards the end of the story, when Havelok is finally able to command a following of warriors, he proceeds with dispatch to return and regain his land and punish his usurpers. It is at this point that the narrative becomes obsessed with feats of arms and the descriptions of the battle scenes reach the stage of the grotesque:

> Hauelok lifte up the dore-tre,
> And at a dint he slow hem thre;
> Was non of hem that his hernes
> Ne lay therute ageyn the sternes.
> The ferthe that he sithen mette,
> Wit the barre so he him grette
> Bifore the heued that the rith eye
> Vt of the hole made he fleye,
> And sithe clapte him on the crune
> So that he stan-ded fel thor dune.
> The fifte that he ouertok
> Gaf he a ful sor dint ok
> Bitwen the sholdres, ther he stod,
> That he spende his herte blod.
> The sixte wende for to fle,
> And he clapte him with the tre
> Rith in the fule necke so
> That he smot hise necke on to.
>
> (1806-1823)

We are meant to sense a turnabout in Havelok's fortunes in these explosions of violence and to realize that, having married and established a band of retainers, he is close to fulfilling his calling. The narration is no longer like love-romance. We are reading a *chanson de geste*.

Yet the political theme that such a change in fortune should suggest gets lost. The poet delves into the grotesque when the subject approaches the socially problematic. Similarly, the poet not only fails to resist the temptation of comedy but indulges in comedy at precisely those moments when either tenderness or piety threaten to overwhelm his narrative, or when the audience is about to be overwhelmed by magic. Havelok is awakened by his suddenly ecstatic wife after she discovers his "kingmark." Later Ubbe's men enjoy the sight of the half-naked

29

couple when they investigate a light coming from the tower in which Havelok and Goldboro are bedded. Saved by a conversation between Grim and Leue, the baby Havelok is dropped on a rock and wishes that he had never been born a king. After Havelok defeats the other participants in a shot-putting contest, they walk away muttering, "We dwellen her to longe!"

Even in the frequent scenes of violence in the poem the horror of what is being described is very often mitigated by an exaggerated scale and an enthusiastic, uncritical tone. Such a style allows a certain evasion. The peculiar moral climate of the poem, in which bloodshed is rendered downright entertaining, is not, I think, a remnant of a healthy paganism. Rather, the blood, gore, and torture of some of these scenes suggest to the audience not naturalism, but a rather naive fantasy world not unlike a modern cartoon or western. The battle scenes, which are meant as references to the battle scenes of epics and *chansons de geste*, are devoid of criticism, moral imperative, or martial excitement, for the vigor and frequent zaniness of the description tend to reduce either our delight at Havelok's revenge or our horror at a peaceful scene being destroyed. For the moment, we are drawn into a cheerful nihilism, by which destruction imposes its own effect, a holiday from morality, resembling comedy.

The poem ends on a utopian note that at the same time recalls the chronicle mode in which the poem opened, for we began as we end, with a perfect government. The poet becomes a recorder, and his record is truth, though one that we might only hope for were we the poet's contemporaries. The irony is that having seen how such a union and such a kingdom might come about, a medieval audience could well throw up its hands, for there is no human way to organize and will helpful angels, magic flames, and incredible coincidences. In a sense, then, the serious political advice, even the indirect criticism, that is contained in the prologue to the poem is compromised.[9]

THE WORLD OF *Havelok* never seems particularly amenable to human will. Even the markedly realistic details for which it has so often been praised are communicated in such a qualified way that we are rarely impressed with the poem's handling of physical reality. Instead, the mind of the reader backslides, concentrating on miracles and gruesome or bizarre images. For the poet too the integration of epic themes with the genre scenes that he too is fond of is accomplished only at moments, and then, only with the aid of magic and dreams:

> Herkne nou hwat me haueth met!
> Me thouthe y was in Denemark set,
> But on on the moste hil
> That euere yete kam i til.
> It was so hey, that y wel mouthe
> Al the werd se, als me thouthe.
> Als i sat upon that lowe,
> I bigan Denemark for to awe,
> The borwes and the castles stronge;
> And mine armes weren so longe
> That i fadmede, al at ones,
> Denemark, with mine longe bones;
> And thanne y wolde mine armes drawe
> Til me, and hem for to haue,
> Al that euere in Denemark liueden
> On mine armes faste clyueden;
> And the stronge castles alle
> On knes bigunnen for to falle;
> The keyes fellen at mine fet.—
> Another drem dremede me ek:
> That ich fley ouer the salte se
> Til Engeland, and al with me
> That euere was in Denemark lyues
> But bondeman and here wiues;
> And that ich kom til Engelond,
> Al closede it intil min hond,
> And, Goldeborw, y gaf it the . . .
> (1285-1311)

Throughout the narrative we are aware of various patterns that seem at some points to dominate the story. There is the theme

31

of political destiny. Then there are striking and successful localized pictures of domestic life, rare in medieval romance and therefore valued perhaps more by modern readers than the author might have intended. Finally there is the *Märchen*-like progress of the hero, which connects the story to fairy tale. But only at certain points in the narrative, which tend to be revelations, as in this dream, does the style rise to any great imaginative power and connect with ease the themes of magic, cabbages, and kings. The dream acts as a unifying device. We know, after Goldboro's commentary on Havelok's dream, not only what their destiny will be but also how the Cinderella theme is connected to the historical imperative, the union of Denmark and England.

In a series of delightfully linked wonders, all occurring on Havelok's and Goldboro's wedding night, Havelok's description of his dream stands out. To prevent Goldboro from having a claim to the throne, the wicked Godrich marries her to a commoner who has achieved renown in the land for his deeds of strength and kindness. Distraught by her new social position, surrounded by commoners with "hors and net, and ship on flode," who brag of their gold and silver, who promise to wash her clothes and bring her water, she lies awake at night, realizing that she has been deceived, when suddenly a beam of light blazes out of the mouth of her new husband. She is now, of course, more terrified than ever, but the voice of an angel tells her that this means her husband is king and she shall be queen after all. At this, with a change of heart, she embraces and kisses her comfortably sleeping mate, who awakes and tells her his dream.

As I have shown in detail above, the narrative has placed great emphasis on geography. But this dream shrinks the entire known world into a surrealistic, iconlike single scene. In this one dream Havelok as king stretches out his arms and, from the hill he imagines himself on, is able to embrace the castles and cities of Denmark. On the night of his actual marriage he also dreams of a mystical political marriage, of the king and his land.[10] As we learn from the second dream, in which Havelok flies to Denmark and brings back all of the land in his hand and gives it to Goldboro, she too plays a political as well as romantic role. Havelok's vision is as much a love song as it is a dream of empire. One reason why this dream is so fascinating is that it seems to have other medieval parallels. The geographic detail that the poet of *Havelok* imparts in the course of his story is touching and naive, but the fantastic scale of this dream is sophisticated and accomplished. The literary models for dream visions were no doubt more sophisticated than those for the representation of reality. The overarching perspective, the point of view of the dreamer from a height far above the world, is a common one in medieval dream tradition. The dream combines perspective, geography, prophecy, and apocalypse. In addition, the figure of the hero reaching halfway across the world, embracing oceans and cities, is not unlike those on icons of royalty in the visual arts. Finally, the delicate tone of Havelok's description resembles that of a love lyric:

> And, Goldeborw, I gaf it the:
> Deus! Lemman, hwat may this be?

Medieval love poetry often combines visual images in a similarly elusive fashion, but the combination is significant here because the poet assumes such an intimate style to communicate information of potentially monumental significance.

The fact remains that the style of this spatially fantastic dream is more accomplished and striking than the style used in presenting the realistic, localizing details for which the poet is so often praised. It is as if the narrator is more concerned with lifting Havelok out of the mire of day-to-day existence than he is in exploring the literary possibilities of that existence. The *Havelok*-poet is not a realist in the sense of dealing seriously with the everyday or the socially problematic. *Havelok* brings a touch of grace to the lives of fishermen, wrestlers, and merchants. It does not draw its grace from them.

Auerbach has conjectured that the breadth and sense of freedom of movement in the Germanic epics derived from the fact that their historical setting was in the period of tribal migrations, so that, compared to later narratives, "the spaces about the

33

occurrences and the heaven above them are incomparably wider
. . . and the structure of society is not so rigidly established."[11]
Narratives such as the *Roland*, for their part, seem constricted,
limited in their settings, with distinct, parceled scenes, resulting
in a structure reflecting feudal political forces. What can such
suggestions tell us about *Havelok*? True, the alignments of its
characters might be seen as a "post-feudal" alliance of king and
commons against the barons, but that does not explain its form
and movement.[12] Rather, its uncertain locus of action and its
backgrounds, which vary from the realistic to the schematic,
indicate a wariness, perhaps unconscious, on the part of the poet
as to where the weight of his action should lie. Neither the
court nor the street seems powerful enough to sustain the pre-
sentation of the world by itself. The social forces that we can
now identify in the poem—urbanization and mercantilization—
seem to have crept into its structure almost by accident.

The poet's seriousness, or at least what he considers as po-
tentially serious in his material, is made clear in the opening
section describing the death of Aethelwold. The poet's com-
ments are political and social, attempting to bring the poem into
a kind of history. Although such themes are not immediately
subverted by his narrative style, it is worth noting that although
the poet can sustain a heightened tone when he wants to, he is
a nervous entertainer. When he thinks his audience is tiring of
high seriousness, or when he tires of it, he switches his tone
in an alarmingly adroit, almost apologetic fashion. Similarly,
the poem at first exhibits a well-planned structure. One could
mark off divisions in the poem, using the frequent summaries
of the plot that the poet includes, something like chapters or
books; but gradually, we, and the narrator, lose sight of such
ordering, and episode piles upon episode, climax upon climax.
We lose the sense of history that the poet establishes at first
and have only a denouement that reverses the trials of—how
many?—years. I emphasize these structural patterns less to be
critical than to underline the themes that the poet himself con-
sidered important. In fact, paying attention to such "epic" ele-
ments in *Havelok the Dane* corrects the excess attention critics

have paid to the story's charm or "Cinderella" theme. That is what the poet does best. But it is not all he has tried to do, and it is not all he has done. The narrative pays due attention to epic and potentially tragic themes and aspires, however awkwardly, to some status as a monumental poem. That the miniature and the comic should be what we value the poem for is certainly not what the poet intended. Yet that disparity is part of *Havelok's* fascination as a narrative.

The sensory realism in the scenes of Grim fishing, Grim's barnyard, and Havelok working in the streets of Lincoln (for the realism of the story is limited to this series of episodes) is energetic and exuberant, but that energy is explosive, and neither the poet nor the rhetorical means he has at hand have much idea what to do with it. We become conscious, on the one hand, of these images of real life. On the other hand, the actual narrative seems to be indulging in the machinery of monumental epic. Yet the poet seems to lack the means to integrate the two. However much we explain this distance in terms of medieval rhetoric or medieval "perspective," the fact remains that the poem is attempting to harness energies for which the literary means have not yet been perfected.

Only at moments of revelation, as we have seen, is there even an uneasy alliance between the marvelous, the epic, and the realistic elements of the poem. The coordination is possible because, as Dieter Mehl has pointed out in another context, the poet borrows more from the typical saint's life than he does from the typical romance.[13] Indeed, one could find the basis of Havelok's cartoonlike humor in any number of saints' lives. But it may also be that the saint's life illustrates in a similar way the workings of the supernatural in a setting that is entirely mundane. So indeed does the *Grettisaga*, and so, to some extent, do folk tales. The *Havelok*-poet's problem is the opposite: he must invest the everyday with a sense of wonder. It may well be that there is some stylistic or structural debt by the *Havelok*-poet to folk tales or saints' lives. But it may also be that such an artful contrast of the mundane and the miraculous is an obvious solution to a common medieval literary problem. The aesthetic result of such a narrative style is to reflect the light that comes from royalty or the supernatural onto the lives of fishermen, peasants, villagers, and the humble apparatus of works and days.

Although there is no character development as such in the narrative, there is a hint of growth, a step towards characters having some strength of their own outside simple narrative functions. Havelok does seem to undergo an education fit for a king, growing from childlike fear to strength and bravery and love.[14] He experiences the conditions of life of all the various social castes that he will rule. Reversals of loyalty are common. Godard and Godrich both turn against their sworn oaths and rationalize their actions in soliloquies. Goldboro, who grows from a baby to a rather haughty young princess, at first despises Havelok, then loves him, in a scene which displays at least as keen a sense of sexual comedy as Chaucer and Chrétien, when she discovers his royal origins. Grim and Leue, whose plight is first rationalized in sociological terms, also turn their allegiance from Godard to Havelok. Grim, Leue, and Goldboro, however, change their minds only when Havelok's mouth shoots its magic flame. And Havelok, no matter what his experience, will still be a king, for kings, in this poem, are born and marked, not made or taught. These attempts at character development, too brief to be convincing, represent an impulse on the part of the poet to invent psychological explanations for that which is already explained by destiny.

Nor is there the attention to tone we can find in a number of other medieval narratives, most specifically those of the alliterative school, but also such romances as *King Horn*. The *Havelok*-poet's art is closer to the art of the preacher, reaching here to the abstruse qualifications of theological speculation, there to the popular and coarse joke.[15] Indeed, the pulpit "stance" of the common preacher, explaining to an often unlettered following, and hence conscious of when the common or the abstract is heading too far in one direction, is analogous to the stance that *Havelok*'s narrator takes. The desire for both ale and salvation is thrown together in the final words of the poem, in a not entirely irreligious or parodic combination of the human and the eternal.

Thus it appears that the voice of the narrator, in however primitive a fashion, begins in *Havelok the Dane* to take on far greater aesthetic importance than in most romances. It may well be that when romance as a narrative form broke beyond the class boundary that originally defined it, it required, to hold it together, a voice rather than a class ethic and idealized ethos, for in the place of the sophisticated and graceful voice of poets such as Chrétien, we begin to sense a more earnest and anxious narrative stance, less confident, though not without irony, humor, and self-awareness. The development of such a voice is not without importance for the poetry of the next century, especially that of Chaucer.

King Horn shares with *Havelok the Dane* a common theme of the young heir orphaned and exiled, who gradually builds a following and returns to claim his birthright, enact revenge, and rule with his queen, whom he has met in the course of his adventures. There are ways in which *King Horn*, however, might be considered the more successful narrative. Its tone, movement, and texture seem more consistent than those of *Havelok the Dane*. Yet the cost of such cohesion is a peculiar disparity of scale, for its "epic" theme is communicated in a nearly lyrical style and a notably restricted representation of reality, for it must exclude or only briefly sketch the background life that, however uneasily integrated, lends *Havelok* its unique charm. At the same time, its form and style reveal many of the same restrictions we noted in the other narrative.

What we would consider the most striking scene in *King Horn* was no doubt the same as the one to which medieval audiences were attracted. A later ballad expands this one scene.[16] The motif itself, the hero disguised as a beggar returning to claim his rightful place, is at least as old as Homer. The use of the crucial feast, with any number of unexpected results, is common in medieval literature. But the tones that the poet heightens

37

are of a particular quality. Here is Horn's speech, when Rymenhild, a good hostess, comes to pour his wine:

> "Quen so dere,
> Wyn nelle ihc muche ne lite
> Bute of cuppe white.
> Thu wenest i beo a beggere,
> And ihc am a fissere,
> Wel feor icome bi este
> For fissen at thi feste:
> Mi net lith her bi honde,
> Bi a wel fair stronde.
> Hit hath ileie there
> Fulle seue yere.
> Ihc am icome to loke
> Ef eni fiss hit toke.
> Ihc am icome to fisse:
> Drynke null y of dyssh:
> Drink to Horn of horne:
> Feor hic am iorne."
>   (1130-1146)

Rymenhild does not recognize this veiled reference to a dream she had many years ago, though the language is so elliptical one wonders whether Horn expects her to remember. He seems to be playing a game with language, equating the reality of his test and return with the magic of dreams. A few lines later he drops the ring that she gave him long ago into the cup. Is it possible she suspects this is Horn? Why does he put off his revelation and so torture her? To test her faith? To protect her? Why does he wait until she is on the brink of suicide? These are questions that might well be asked of epics and of longer romances, but not with much fruitfulness of *King Horn*. If such motivations and tensions are intended by our poet, he is suggesting them only in the most allusive fashion, in the fashion of ballads. The poet combines the world of dreams and symbols with the world of action. At the center of the poem is this remarkable recognition scene, but a recognition obscured by a disguise, a dream, the long forgotten details of that dream, and by the evocative symbolism of the ring and the cup. If we wish to see dramatic action in these few lines, it is there. Rymenhild, dutiful and resigned, passes the cup of wine and listens to Horn's puzzling speech. Her calm disturbed, she asks him about King Horn, and he gives her the ring. Her hopes suddenly raised, she asks him where he got the ring, but he tells her that Horn is dead. Crushed, she contemplates suicide. Horn, however, reveals himself in time. But all this happens so quickly that what we are impressed with is not the structure and irony of this dramatic plot or the delay of their inevitable reunion, but with the magic created by the intercourse of symbols and narrative crises and with the sudden and surprising adroitness of the poetry, Horn's pun on his own name, and the many possible meanings of "fish." The poet succeeds in weaving together the effects of two sorts of structure, one radically linear—the narrative itself—the other symbolic and evocative—the epiphany of a lyric. I think the struggle of scholars to find evidence of other genres as models for *King Horn* is an attempt to account for this confluence of lyric and narrative.[17] The problem is that the poet has accomplished such a dual effect by reducing his narrative scale to that of a ballad. As a result, the poem impresses us with a large number of local successes, but the larger narrative movement, which should frame the importance of such local moments, remains flimsy and one-dimensional.

Horn's speeches in this later part of the poem are in keeping with his speeches throughout the narrative, consisting of little more than announcements of who he is and how he got there. Now, however, these announcements are overlaid with layers of disguise, plotting, and indirectness. The poetic magic of these later speeches, compared to Horn's pedestrian remarks in the earlier part of the story, have something to do with this new element. Essentially, his major speeches remain identity and travel reports. At first (201), he announces himself and his travels simply and clearly. Gradually, as his world becomes more complex, he resorts to indirection, becoming Cutberd, an adventuring knight (767). Finally, close to his return and re-

39

venge, when he can soon reveal himself simply as Horn again, he tells us his usual information, in the lines I have quoted above, in a baroque veil of language. He is a beggar. No, he is a fisherman. No, he is a companion of Horn. And each time the language he uses keeps him this side of duplicity, making the half-lies more accurate than the actual fact. Again, the content of his speeches remains the same—who he is and where he came from—but such information becomes more and more indirect and elusive.

There is a degree of almost artistic complexity in Horn's return that is lacking in nearly all other early Middle English romances. It bespeaks a kind of self-assurance, indeed, a self-consciousness, that plays nicely against the anonymity of Horn's situation and the quest for identity that is at least suggested by the plot. For a similar kind of self-consciousness and complexity we need to turn either to the elaborate self-testing of the hero in earlier French romance or to the actions of the often otherworldly adversary in later Middle English romance. There is something uncanny about Horn's return, a mood that is emphasized by the lyrical quality of the verse in this section and the elusive play on names and words. There is nothing of this in other early Middle English romances. When the magic flame shoots out of Havelok's mouth, he is barely aware of it and is slightly puzzled by Goldboro's newfound enthusiasm; Havelok's return is marked by force and will rather than wit and ingenuity. In *Havelok* we are made to feel at one with both hero and nation, though like his people, we develop more and more respect for the hero as he matures. In *Horn*, however, those background characters are minimized and there is a certain association of the reader with the wit and intelligence of the hero. In any case, there is a resemblance between the resources of the hero and the poet, who seems able to recombine his repertoire of conventions in often original and unlikely ways.

One clear observation, which the last scenes in *King Horn* bear out, is that the setting up of the action, the maneuvering of characters from place to place, takes up just as much room as the action itself. Indeed, even the scene of Horn's return and

revenge partakes of the same narrative pattern that dominates
the poem. First, we have the questions raised by Rymenhild
and the cryptic answers by Horn. Then the action moves quickly
back and forth among minor settings, with a great many sketchy
directions through the bare space of the poem. First, "the Quen
yede to bure / With hire maidenes foure" (1163-1164). There
she examines the ring: "Tho sente heo a damesele / After the
palmere" (1169-1170). She asks him where he got the ring and
he tells her the false story of Horn's death. When she faints,
Horn reveals himself and gives her the right story. Horn leaves:
" 'Rymenhild,' he sede, 'y wende / Adun to the wudes ende.' "
Then, "Horn sprong vt of halle." Meanwhile, "The Quen yede
to bure / And fond Athulf in ture." She repeats what we have
just been told, at which "Athulf bigan to springe / For the
tithinge: / After Horn he arnde anon." Again we have a mes-
senger with information, a small change of scene, a revelation
that revises that information, another shift of scene; then a new
character is told what has transpired, and the primary action is
finally precipitated. Such a chain reaction becomes a minor ac-
tion in itself, and we can only assume that the poet intended
us to be at least as interested in such complications as in the
heroic action itself, as he certainly seems to be. Nor does such
a pattern offer artfulness or suspense; rather, it simplifies the
narrative. The characters move like wind-up toys, jerkily mov-
ing here and there, setting each other in motion. For all the
local directions, the space they move in seems to be a vacuum.
We have no sense of distance or of real movement. The "woods"
and "tower" are barely mentioned enough to exist in our minds
as mental props. Instead, the narrative depends on an element
of time, of getting everything together at the proper moment
to carry on the rescue, and everything else seems to rush for-
ward at once to that end, collapsing as it does. Despite the scenes
of love and war we expect from the poem, its primary move-
ments are neither those of simple battle arrangements or elab-
orate courting rituals. Rather, the most important scenes are
of two people talking, dealing in secrets, disclosures, and re-

minders. The poem is more about communication than it is about conflict.

The narrative style of the poem often seems to be a mechanical system of shorthand that we must suppose, the audience could fill in. Scenic indications are so abbreviated that they seem to be notes that will be expanded upon later in the poem, but such completion never occurs. One would like to think that the poet is overextending the traditional signs and conventions of a romance lexicon that we have unfortunately lost. But Chaucer could be cruel with abbreviated romance conventions in *Sir Thopas*. Here, instead of drawing contingent detail quickly to leave room for that which is central, everything is reduced to a score.

The narrative indications of space and time, the transitions between episodes, and the ways in which characters are moved about the canvas of this poem all contribute to the poem's one-dimensional impression, and this thinness is shared by much else in *King Horn*. The sense of social reality that *Havelok the Dane* projects, however partially, is here represented only in schema or in disguise. Horn at crucial points in the story dons various disguises, all of which are perfectly conventional. As the knight Cutberd, he is traveling to "seche mine beste," which among its meanings might well have a slight commercial overtone, though its meaning is vague enough to describe Horn's true mission. At other times he becomes a beggar, a pilgrim, and a minstrel. The importance of these conventional disguises is that they allow Horn to travel freely over the world of this poem, moving from place to place in ways that do not call into question the sketchy spatial indications of the narrative. We construct the vertical dimension of society not by any details or by the influence of everyday life on the circumstances of the plot, but by Horn's own identity as a king and his disguise as a knight seeking his fortune, as a palmer, and as a minstrel.

The often mechanical narrative techniques of *King Horn* are related to its balladic quality. In ballads transitions between episodes are usually understood rather than stated; scenes are simply juxtaposed. In *King Horn* fairly exact directions may be given to tell us where specific characters are located. But since their movements are so frequent and jerky, they seem more like the figures of ballads than those of more extensive narratives. Typically, the pattern of their movements follows a distinct paradigm. The narrator describes an action by one of the main characters. Then that character goes on his or her way to another place, where he or she meets another character. A conversation ensues, which generally consists of no more than the first character telling the second precisely what the narrator has already told us. This usually results in a new impulse to action, and the cycle begins again.

This pattern imposes certain strictures on the narrative. For one thing, it forces a major character such as Horn to do little else but talk about how he got where he is. An astonishing number of Horn's lines consist of little besides describing his origin and destination. Certainly such repetition occurs in *Havelok* and in any number of other romances, but in *King Horn* the poet seems hypnotized by the pattern and often seems to owe his allegiance first to the continuation of that pattern and then to the elucidation of his themes. At one of the crucial turning points in the story, for instance, Horn learns that Rymenhild is about to be married. He is told by a messenger who bears a letter from Athulf. The actual process of communication, however, is more complex than the situation requires. The context involves the refusal of Horn to marry Reynild, the king's daughter, because he has already promised himself to Rymenhild. But he remains in that land, disguised as Cutberd, "Fulle seue yere," during which, since the time he has killed the Saracen giant, nothing of importance seems to have happened. In point of fact, nothing does happen during this period. The passage of time is not merely adumbrated, as in epics, but elided, as in ballads. Now, in lines 923-929, we learn that Rymenhild is threatened by an unfortunate marriage. In lines 930-936 Athulf sends his messengers out in search of Horn. In lines 937-942 Horn himself comes upon one of the messengers and asks him what he is looking for. In lines 943-966 the same information given in 923-929 is repeated. In lines 961-966 Horn reveals himself and promises to return, thus providing the messenger with new information. The messenger must now return home with this new message, taking the locus of action with him.

Irony and tension are produced in *King Horn* by disrupting the expected pattern I have outlined above. The messenger, armed with the crucial information that Horn has given him, ought to go back and repeat that information to Athulf or Rymenhild. But instead his body washes onto the shore near Rymenhild's castle. On the level of narrative continuity the audience must ask those questions that the plot demands. What will Rymenhild, who is after all prone to extreme behavior, do to keep her promise? Will Horn return in time?

That is to say, in *King Horn*, time and place are largely represented by action and gesture. True, the chronology of the narrative is more or less biographical—its plot is the span of Horn's life. But by no means do we have anything resembling the personal consciousness of time, that marks later narratives such as *Sir Gawain and the Green Knight* or earlier narratives such as those of Chrétien, where the isolation of the hero from the court introduces us to both a new world outside that court and a new awareness and growth on the part of the hero. In *King Horn* the swift transitions take us from place to place with little sense of duration, and the result is an impression that the world is relatively static, waiting only to be betrayed or stolen by villains like Fikenhild or the Saracens or saved by heroes like Horn. Except for this initial fall and this eventual salvation, all else seems to be only a momentary tableau, created by the swift entrance of the central characters and broken by their exit, presumably to return to some kind of stasis. From a sheerly aesthetic point of view, this situation can only be regarded as inferior to the growth of character and consciousness in twelfth-century chivalric romance or the narrative control of some poets in the following century. But as a social configuration, it speaks to a sense of attempted mastery over the world, of energy and control, though with an admittedly shaky confidence that forestalls too many unsettling questions.

If the geography of the poem is drawn for us by the frequent journeys of its characters and by Horn's adoption of traveler's disguises, that too is schematic,[18] for the journeys never seem to take us anywhere. The world remains the same bare set, with only the names changed. Whatever is exotic in the poem, some of its travels or its unreal Saracens, none of these involve or express its audience's geographical, historical, or philosophical awareness. Whatever in the poem approaches an ethical or a social problem becomes merely a momentary puzzlement, to be immediately resolved. That the hero should finally, with his men, be dressed as entertainers, "Hi sede, hi weren harpurs, / And sume were gigours," is itself significant.

But the limited perspectives of *King Horn* are by no means a flawed version of realism. They are in fact a version of reality. Things do happen again and again, but such repetition in *King Horn* has its point too. It keeps before us always a double interpretation of the plot, one public and social, the other private and individual. That few such moments are integrated (as in *Havelok*, too) reflects the conception of reality in these narratives. In both earlier and later romances, the spheres of public and private concerns are shown to be in conflict, and their resolution is a chief source of interest in the narrative. Here, they seem to be mastered separately, and the contradictions, though marked, are minimized.

It is almost as if the spareness of the diction were to be compensated by the multiplication of incidents and the repetition of motifs. We are to look for the richness of the work, that is, not in the texture of the individual phrase or line, but in the larger collocations of the narrative and the juncture of scenes and themes. This is of course part of the art of oral and formulaic poetry as described by many scholars, but I see no reason why it might not also be an effect to be sought by a lettered poet working in a literary tradition of limited vocabulary. Even the words we can identify as loan words are of the most conventional sort and are used not so much to vary or render description exotic as to make everything immediately comprehensible without savoring the strangeness of word or phrase. Unlike some

45

other romancers, the poet of *Horn* seems to have understood the power inherent in such simplicity, and in many ways his style is less condescending than far frailer narratives dressed in rhetorically elaborate trappings. Although complicated descriptions in French chivalric romance are significant forms that generate their own meaning, the class and ethical validity of that meaning is missing for an English audience. And the powers of narrative—movement, dynamism, large actions that move between discrete (and class determined) places and courts—are of more importance.

At the same time that the plot of *King Horn* concerns danger and disaster, its style, in an occasionally musical and always repetitive fashion, suggests a kind of safety. Incidents and phrases follow in an almost incantatory way so that the eventual triumph of good is made to seem inevitable and the potentially threatening dangers—the Saracens, usurpations, war—tend to strengthen rather than threaten the values of the poem. Although its action occasionally verges on epic, its form is clearly that of romance, with its emphasis on identity and social ritual. The great battle scenes of epic open up a broad vista, a vision of the world that includes rather than excludes a variety of human and superhuman experience. For all its battle and bluster, however, *King Horn* presents a closed world. We tend not to relive the incidents of the plot. Description is pared. Instead, we are referred to our own knowledge in such incidents; we are forced to translate the code of *King Horn* into experience.[19] But since such experience is the highly ritualized discourse of court life, the poem becomes a kind of metalanguage.

This is not to condemn works such as *King Horn* for what they do not promise, but to indicate that the consideration of major themes, of politics, and of the world, as in *Havelok the Dane*, and the relationship of the human and the ultimate in the best narratives of the thirteenth century is extremely limited. There seems to be no way, at least in early Middle English romance, to treat such themes in the proper key. In the next century narrative poets could begin to exploit a sense of crisis, but the best of these early Middle English romances offered

46

their audience a perspective that precluded rather than encouraged serious questions.

AUERBACH HAS SHOWN us how the chivalric romances present the world as class fantasies, where everything is merely a background for a chivalric ethic and where problematic details of life are excluded, perhaps because they are beginning to threaten the continued hegemony of that ethic. But the early Middle English romances seem to base their appeal on a broader, less exclusive, but equally fantastic escape: they project a world and people it with characters who retain the appeal and innocence of youth but little of youth's dependence and petulance and who experience the adventure and romance of the adult, but with none of its compromises or disappointments. Return and reunion for these characters never involves the recognition of an innocence lost, for their England, or Denmark, has not changed. It is never really very clear, except by careful inference, how long they have been gone. They do not grow in maturity by facing crises; they merely react to another danger, which can be overcome by another strategy. Conflicts of value, between love and valor, between individual desire and social responsibility, must be read into these early romances.

Dorothy Everett long ago pointed out one of the primary differences between French and English romances:

> In the romance, the plot may be elaborate and complicated, is often rambling and often interrupted by long descriptive passages or accounts of the hero's feelings (particularly in the French romances of Chrétien de Troyes). . . . Compared with the tale, the romance can be clumsy, vague, and discursive, but at its best there is a breadth of view about it. Whereas the teller of a tale goes straight forward, looking neither to right nor left, the romance writer "dwells on the circumstantial.". . . The romance offers a more difficult and dangerous road to success than the tale.[20]

I doubt whether Everett meant such a distinction to be truly generic. But it is a commonplace of literary history that Middle

English romancers were more concerned with the *tale* than were their French masters. More often than not, the reason given for such a difference is that the English versions were taking a literary shortcut, or that their audience, less urbane, thirsted for adventure and plot. The "circumstantial" in the case of the French romances consisted of the conflict among pure ideals in the mind of the chivalric hero, the catalogue of the trappings of aristocratic life, or graceful descriptions that reflected the delicacy of a perfect courtly consciousness. To an English audience with a broader class mixture, all these might well have become either exotic, or fraught with contradiction for those who were removed from court life and who aspired to the more attainable fixtures of a class above them.[21] It is significant that in the romances we have looked at in this chapter the hero is not in search of ideal perfection, but merely the attainment of what is by rights his. He does not have time to grow weary of his reward; indeed, he hardly has time to use it. Thus escape for English audiences meant not a fantasy world based on aristocratic chivalry, but a world in which those values produce satisfaction and not conflict.

Horn and Havelok are at peace only in the introduction and conclusion. The rest of the story maintains a constant sense of crisis, which, admittedly, they meet with increasing control. The segments of their lives that we see in these romances take place in a historical vacuum, a world in which history is willing to wait for the hero to act. Such an ideal stasis is mirrored in the abstraction of the time locations and backgrounds that I have described above.

It is not merely a matter of increased syntactic flexibility that distinguishes the sense of continuity in Chaucer and *Sir Gawain and the Green Knight* from the relatively episodic quality of earlier romances. Certainly there is a strong element of quantitative, "Gothic" structure in the latter poets. But the sense of flow, subordination, and connection of incidents is far stronger in the fourteenth-century poets. Even when their poems display a formalized, structured architecture, that architecture is dazzlingly reflected and refracted into facets, as if to encourage continuity and relationships. The great mass of noncyclic romances, however, despite their liveliness, are built of a far more ritualized language, even when the level of diction of that language is popular. Indeed, the puzzle of these romances derives at least in part from their social imagery, full of vitality at least as compared to their French predecessors, encased in a stylistic tradition that seems to keep incidents, images, and background material distinct. The reasons for this—figural connections, oral residue, or "immaturity"—are less central to our concern here than what this reveals about the reception and social import of the romances, with a relatively dynamic content in a fixed form.

A reduction in conventional descriptive passages and epic devices, the "circumstantial," has been explained as a function of the rationalization supposedly characteristic of English taste. This may well be true, but closer to the root of the problem are those scholars who have pointed out that Middle English audiences had a class basis less limited than the court, which probably contained bourgeois elements. This did not necessarily mean a reduction in taste. Rather, the romances seem to manifest a reduction in *perspective*: elements of history, impressions of geography (however fantastic), scenes that celebrate the literacy of both audience and character, all these have been eliminated. This information often emphasized to a particular and limited audience why this story was being told to them, but such an approach was not appropriate for a broader audience. Just as the indications of time tend to be vague in the Middle English romances, the physical world of these narratives is remarkably homogeneous.

Many early Middle English romances celebrate the expansion of the geographic world that followed upon the crusades and the new trade routes. They shift their locales back and forth to register that expansion, but their "worlds" remain oddly enclosed. It is a fact of their narrative technique that the most important and revelatory scenes occur not where this new geographical imagination could inform the action, but in towers, in bedrooms, in cottages, in dining halls. The real literary exploitation of new worlds is minimal, as if a modern film were to be made based on a plot that hopped from London to Paris to Moscow to New York to New Delhi to Ghana to Rio but always took place in an airport, international style, steel and glass. This effect of insularity in Middle English romance depends not only on the fact that the major scenes take place inside conventional enclosures but also on the fact that the transitions that take us through this world remain so sketchy.

If we revise our preconception that the essence of romance should lie in chivalric quest, which demands some mastery of movement and transition, then the abbreviated transitional scenes in *Havelok* and *King Horn* with their often confusing geography and their mysteriously passing periods of days, even years, become less of a flaw. The essential scenes of the narrative are never those that idealize knightly behavior, for these, in our examples, are more decorative forms that have degenerated into insignificance. The distension of such scenes into the comic or the grotesque is evidence of this. Instead, the crucial scenes of these early Middle English romances are scenes of revelation and communication. The skills that thus become of importance are dramatic skills, controlling how characters confront one another and what the meaning of that confrontation is. This incidental development of dramatic skill may well be an effort on the part of the poet to compensate for an aesthetic that apparently ignored the essential qualities of narrative: subordination, causality, structure, continuity. The normal tendency of a writer to fill in is fulfilled in these early Middle English romances by packing the narrative with scenes of characters engaged in conversations in lieu of a climax arrived at by the sheer force of linear inevitability.

Clearly these poets learn how to make their characters explain themselves in monologue and so forth from the tradition of Chrétien. But when the characters in Chrétien's romances come together, they elaborate on the problems of courtly love and knightly honor.[22] In Middle English romance the characters come together to speak but have forgotten what to say (or so we might imagine a member of Chrétien's audience might think). The speeches, which ought to involve the *meaning* of their actions, only reassert the *role* of the characters. Hence King Horn talks always about who he is and where he has come from; hence Havelok always reminds himself of his duty.

These romances, then, have a "progressive" structural arrangement, in which characters come together to analyze and explain their motivations, which Vinaver sees as part of the "discovery of meaning." In Chrétien, and in the *Gawain*-poet and in Chaucer, the characters who compose these patterns, however much they may be types, are at least capable of undergoing and verbalizing biographical experience. But the early Middle English romancers have inserted characters into this pattern who seem not to be conscious of this function, who remain vague, who lack introspection, perhaps because, as I have suggested, they embody synthesis and not conflict.[23]

But this criticism ignores the importance of such dialogues in the value system of the work, for their real meaning is not in the message they carry, but in the social network they generate. That is, the interest of early Middle English romance is not the incipient development of individual character as we observe it in high French romance. Instead, it is the relationship of characters to the usually royal hero that becomes the center of our attention. This is markedly different from earlier courtly romances. There, our attention is usually on a high noble (rarely a royal personage), and the point of his speeches, or significantly, soliloquies, is to explore a conflict between his individual desire and social obligation. In this exploration is the germ of what we regard as character or individual personality. But such a contradiction is relatively minimal in *Horn* and *Havelok*. Their real problem is to reveal themselves to their followers and to mobilize them, and it is this system of loyalties that defines them.

In French chivalric romances a basic pattern asserts itself time after time. The knight sets forth and engages in a series of fantastic adventures. These adventures may be the only way in which a member of his class could carry out his traditional function. Or they may represent a test of chivalric values in an extreme context from which he, and his values, return trium-

51

phant. That is, one can regard chivalric romance as absurd heroism or as a purification and reassertion of class values. Although the earliest romances in English retain the basic pattern of quest, adventure, return, and reintegration, they adapt this pattern, as it were, devoid of class content. Paradoxically, this means that there is more class mixture and more assimilation of everyday life. The heroes are no less exalted, but their situation is not nearly as much that of an elite. Indeed, their adventures are often abbreviated and speeches clipped so that the significant scenes seem to be those of communication with confidants, servants, and citizens. Although such a pattern is a lesson in good kingship, it also suggests that the audience of the romance might be composed of accessory members of society. The hero of chivalric romance eventually is (triumphantly) reintegrated into his social world, but what holds our attention is his problematic alienation from it. The hero of early English romance is kept from his rightful reward, but he is never caught in a contradictory ethical situation and is always surrounded by images of community.

Thus the most interesting characters in these earlier Middle English romances are not the heroes and heroines, but the helping characters, whose involvement in the affairs of the simpler protagonists does involve conflict. In Chrétien, more often than not, the hero and heroine are caught between two ethics or promises: Lancelot, Erec and Enide, Isolde. In the Middle English romances, the duty of the heroes is clear, but the helping characters are caught between.

Compared to any of Chrétien's heroes, or even any of Chaucer's romance heroes, the lack of introspection on the part of heroes like Horn and Havelok is remarkable. Although Horn at least seems capable of acknowledging courtly sentiment, neither poem indulges in such an exploration of aristocratic psychology. The omission says much about the character of the poet's audience, though less perhaps about the skill of the poet than is commonly supposed, but its real impact is on the tenuous connection of theme and narrative form. The bare outline of the plot, involving the usurpation of the hero's birthright and his eventual triumph, suggests a movement towards maturity, that is, a version of coming of age common to romance as a mode. Yet the actual impact of the work as a whole, not least because of some of the local contradictions I have described above, is one of melodramatic suddenness rather than dramatic change. What we remember (even in Havelok's most ruthless moments) is a kind of naiveté, an adolescent and awkwardly ingratiating quality. The historical background of the poem is just that; we return to the pacific ground of the natural world that was unnaturally disturbed by the usurpation, but we have little sense of a change in consciousness or society. Yet for a thirteenth-century audience, the appeal of these narratives seemed to be based on, rather than in spite of, their odd rejection of change and historical process.

It is too easy to say that the form of these romances vitiates the content, and unfair to say that their comic and miniature elements subvert their serious intent. The poets, particularly that of *Havelok*, are involved in a sometimes desperate search for a form that will somehow express important historical issues, despite a language that is neither forceful enough nor subtle enough, despite a verse that constantly opts for the comic or lyric rather than the epic. Hints of grandeur are often at odds with the theme itself. The epic scene is often portrayed in a humorous light. Details and flourishes are allowed to become the center of attention, as if a garden had taken over the building it surrounds. Old English narrative never had such a problem. This is not merely to repeat Ker's dictum that romance was decadent epic. If we are to take these narratives as art, something their commentators and cataloguers have not always been willing to do, we must ask questions about the attitude of the poet and his audience towards the story. Even when these earlier Middle English narrative poets approached their material with seriousness and epic intent, they could not resist questioning the adequacy of that intent. The poet, in collusion with his audience, accepts the limitations, rather than the possibilities—either epic or tragic—of the story.

The qualifications of the epic, the refusal to face the facts of apocalypse that expressed the deepest sense of crisis in medieval consciousness, result in the creation of narratives that, however effective as stories, move towards the timelessness and "no-place" of utopia. Behind this sensibility may well lie a social cause. Class mixture in the audience, perhaps even the presence of a new class who aspired to the poses of the aristocracy, may well have encouraged the spread of what was once a courtly form but discouraged the fine puzzlements and ethical refinements upon which romance in twelfth-century France originally fed. At the same time, these early Middle English romances do not attempt to question the moral, or literary bias of the audience. Instead, they affirm any such prejudices and end in a sense of happy and not at all ironic community. We have no doubt that the poet is on our side.

Such is not the case in the best narratives of the next century.

Disorientation, Style, and Perception in *Sir Gawain and the Green Knight*

Partly because of the emergence of self-consciousness on the part of poets, perhaps because of the defensive position of a poet in a court composed of his social betters, perhaps because of the general sense of cultural crisis in the late fourteenth century, the relationship between narrative art and audience in the best fourteenth-century poetry is markedly different from that in the poetry of a century before. The romances of the thirteenth century allowed the audience to escape the crises and questions that medieval narrative, given its profoundly Christian character, might be expected to plumb. This is not at all what happens in either Chaucer or the *Gawain*-poet. My readings of *Sir Gawain and the Green Knight* and *Troilus and Criseyde* in the following chapters emphasize that, however entertaining, their form and style imply a challenge and even an assault on the sensibilities and shared values of their audience.

We have gotten used to the idea that *Sir Gawain and the Green Knight* is a formally perfect narrative, that much of its effect derives from its exquisite structure and symmetry.[1] Although I do not dispute such a view, I wish to emphasize a countertendency that is equally important in terms of the effect of the narrative on the audience, for the style depends upon subtle disorientation and unbalancing effects. Such effects are obvious on any first reading of the poem but are minimized as we scrutinize the poem's complex web of relationships. The first section of this chapter is a general description of the extent to which the poem includes themes of decline, decadence, disorientation, dismemberment, as well as perfection. The second section explores some specific examples of how the poem's rhetoric disorients the reader in units as small as a stanza. I will describe some of the ways in which the poem's imagery and ironies even call into question the reader's response. The last section of this chapter tries to explain the relationship of all these aspects of style to the consciousness of the audience or reader.

Some of the most interesting recent criticism of *Sir Gawain* has in fact noticed that the narrator of the poem is not always as candid with his audience as he pretends to be. Obviously we do not know that Bercilak and the Green Knight are the same person until the end of the poem. As Donald R. Howard has pointed out, "the Green Knight plays a game with the court, the author plays games with the reader. He goes on hinting that it is all a joke and implying that the reader knows some things which Arthur and his court do not. In part, this is so: it is all preposterous, and we know perfectly well there is a catch to it somewhere. At the same time the author withholds from us just what it is and keeps us guessing."[2] More generally, A. C. Spearing suggests that there are unresolved ambiguities in the poem, for "the poet has given us a richly suggestive concretion of material. That material does not fall of itself into a single pattern of organization and significance, but into a number of alternative patterns. The choice and the adjustment are ours."[3] Other critics have made similar observations about crucial junctures in the poem. Yet it has not been sufficiently emphasized how the style of *Sir Gawain and the Green Knight*, in both its largest and minutest aspects, contributes to a process of disorientation.

THE STYLE of the *Gawain*-poet has been explained by reference to his own phrase, "letteres loken," or by analogy with the interconnected lines of the pentangle on Gawain's shield. But it should also be noted how closely the *Gawain*-poet's literary effects parallel the various dismemberments that take place in the poem—if not the actual decapitation, then at least the highly ritualized butchering of the animals killed in Bercilak's hunt, carefully taken apart and reorganized. The complex structure of *Gawain* often makes us forget how the poem depends on disorientation as much as balance, analysis as much as synthesis. Often the poet presents a scene, and then resolves it into distinct components. His approach to meaning and emotions too is analytic.[4] Gawain's shield is described, then the significance of it brought out, its components listed, parsed, elucidated. Even the character of Gawain is revealed to us at once in the beginning where he is described as a perfect knight. Then gradually the defenses of that role are probed. Gawain's values are taken apart, stripped down. Contradictions appear. (The circumstances surrounding the Green Knight's part of the plot are quite different: the clues are given to us one by one and are only put together at the end.)

The dismemberments we find in *Gawain* are of a substantially different nature from those we find either in epics such as *Beowulf* or in romances such as *Havelok the Dane*. In *Beowulf* there is an utter, primitive horror of dismemberment, as a violation of the sacredness of the body so important in the epic consciousness. The head of Æschere or the arm of Grendel are surreal, horrible images that contrast with the ordered and natural spaces in which they are set. The dismemberments in *Sir Gawain and the Green Knight* are not sacrilege but ritual. The beheading of the Green Knight is described in a style not unlike that of some parts of *Beowulf*, but the circumstances are so entirely different as to suggest a different world view towards such things—not horror but surprise or shock. The reaction is to a lack of decorum rather than to the annihilation of the human image. In *Gawain* there are rules for dismemberment, just as there are rules for the rhetoric that describes so vividly, and with so much enjoyment, the decapitation of the Green Knight and the butchering of the animals.[5] Gawain respects the rules of the beheading game. The animals are butchered by the book. Part of Gawain's quandary is a passive, if perfect, acceptance of the rules that might conceivably lead to his own decapitation.

It is true that the poet's inspired description of Bercilak's castle is derived from a fascination with architectural forms of order. But we are reminded that Gothic architecture, scholasticism, logic, rhetoric, even the analytic style of this poem might have been expressions of the same basic tendency.[6] On the one hand, this mania for dividing and subdividing is an attempt to imitate in microcosm the universal hierarchies of creation. On the other hand, this attempt results in an impossible and utopian frenzy, for the nature of stone is resistant to immateriality. Indeed, the description of the castle in *Sir Gawain*, "pared out of papure purely hit semed," emphasizes this paradox, which is part of the paradox of the plot, the seeking for purity, spirituality, abstraction, in a world earthbound and material.

There is a sense in which, without our being the least bit pejorative, we can read *Sir Gawain and the Green Knight* as a decadent romance. First of all, it reflects an ideal of chivalry that might have been viable two hundred years before. In the fourteenth century, however, such an ideal could at best be a myth. The poem is steeped in the milieu of the late fourteenth century and exhibits that period's preoccupation with ritual and form that encumber rather than encourage action.[7] Life is rendered in visual images each distinct and carefully enumerated, like the details of Flemish landscapes. It is a style aimed less at discovering physical reality than at redeeming it from a habit of mind that would see through all things to a symbolic transcendence. In form, however perfect, the narrative is a tour de force, achieving the sublest of effects within a complex, artful, and at the same time nearly heroic meter. There is an extreme self-consciousness behind all this art.

The *Gawain*-poet loves to draw out the moods of the edges of the day: dawn and dusk. Similarly, he concentrates his significant actions at the edges of the year: the "Nwe yr," for instance, when the two tests occur. His much admired passage on the turn of the seasons is compelling not simply because of the static descriptions of summer, fall, winter, and spring, but because we see the seasons in flux, turning into one another; and the poetry's achievement lies in its suggestion of gradation and change. The poet's imagination is compelled towards blocks—years, days, nights, opponents, objects that face each other—as if the interface between them could bring out some truth or definition that one or the other alone might not possess.

This fascination with beginnings and endings is a fascination at once with the archaic and decadent. The poem itself begins and ends with the same lines, a reference to the epic story of Troy, to the origins both of England and of chivalry. The narrator looks back to a golden age. Gawain is the best knight. The land, except for some occasional respites seems still primeval. But the implication that this was a golden age suggests that civilization has been a falling-off since then, down to a fourteenth-century present. Yet we see Arthur as a boy. We see the court and Gawain in the springtime of their existence. Although there may be a touch of condescension in these portrayals, they do suggest an impulse by an audience and the poet to embrace that lost youth, though the poem ends up gracefully accepting that loss. The love of objects and delicate architecture and the heightening of the senses suggest the opposite of an archaic mentality. Finally, however, the poem reminds us that redemption is possible in terms of the natural history that gives birth to beginnings and endings, and the eternal redemption that transcends them, to which the poem finally turns.

The most widely disparate details are brought within a causal pattern, with an aim to delight and surprise. For all its precision, the poem's meaning remains elusive, and its moral, if it has one, is not always agreed upon by readers.[8] Although it is no doubt an accident of literary history that leaves the poem in its splendid isolation, the fact remains that from it issues no progeny, and the tradition that lies behind it does not prepare us for some of its effects.[9]

The history that is included in the poem is itself ironic. Romance always takes place in an imaginary past, but the past of *Sir Gawain* is peculiarly shifty. Even Arthur's court seems to lack the tone of epic majesty that the invocation to Troy and Brutus suggests. Romulus may have been the legendary founder of medieval knighthood, but Arthur's court seems to be an

59

uncertain inheritor of that mantle. Only to Gawain do the values of a mythical Britain remain alive, and in him, too abstractly. Even in this golden past, the aristocracy expends its energies not on battles or politics, but on feasting and hunting, which are raised to the level of occupations. We are told that they do other things, but all we see is this. The enemies Gawain kills—boars, bulls, giants, dragons—seem hardly a threat to the social order. All we can assume is that they got in his way. Even the moods of the poem—from festivity and childlike daring and excitement to the sublime pessimism of the doomed Gawain—reflect the heightened sensibility of the waning of the Middle Ages.

The settings of the poem also form a significant pattern. If for a moment we ignore the journeys that link Camelot, the castle of Bercilak, and the Green Chapel, we notice a progressive exteriorization of the scenes that contain the major dramatic confrontations. The beheading scene and challenge occur indoors. The temptation scene with the lady is indoors, but it is sandwiched between the hunting scenes, which take place out of doors. Finally, the last test takes place outdoors, in an enchanted area of some sort. Thus the poem moves from architecture, enclosure, and order towards geography, nature, and vulnerability. Even this obvious pattern is fraught with contradictions, for the interiors—the court, bedchamber, and so forth—are the places where the forces of the social world are most intense, even paralyzing. In the outside one can fulfill without conflict one's expected function by slaying giants, boars, and dragons. Or one may, as in the end, exculpate in the outside world the inevitable sins and falls caused by any action in the interior world.

On the other hand, the progressive exteriorization of the action reflects the coming out of the hero, a rejection of both his debutant and illusory status as a perfect knight. It is also a journey into age: the young hero confronted by the markedly older Green Knight or Bercilak, his more sophisticated wife, and the aged hag who lurks in the background. No doubt too the icy landscape around the Green Chapel suggests not only age and winter but death. Surely, however, a more specific point is being made by this exteriorization of the action, for Gawain must now explain his ideals outside of their immediate social context, test them in this timeless landscape, literally outside of the court from which they sprang. Furthermore, he must stand alone, and for all his armor, naked, before a certain judgment, though this one is minor. He must accept a human definition, which underlies his heroic definition of himself. The props of civilization are gone. The encounter, which seems to involve, for the hero, questions of innocence and experience or perfection and decline, is outlined clearly by removing it from the context of those luxurious surroundings that are so often forms of solace. At the end, it is no longer a "new age." We were not as young as we thought.

BENEATH THE splendid formal surface of *Sir Gawain*, then, run certain subversive currents. This counterpoint is not thematic alone. In the structure of certain passages, we can locate a distinct strategy on the part of the poet. He builds up our expectations, using the conventions of rhetoric and romance, then subtly shifts the subject of his discourse away from what our experience would lead us to expect. The result is that the reader is always correcting himself and is quick to take the blame, like the hero, for the deviousness of nature and human nature. The second stanza is a case in point:

> Ande quen this Bretayn watz bigged bi this burn rych,
> Bolde bredden therinne, baret that lofden,
> In mony turned tyme tene that wroghten.
> Mo ferlyes on this folde han fallen here oft
> Then in any other that I wot, syn that ilk tyme.
> Bot of alle that here bult, of Bretaygne kynges,
> Ay watz Arthur the hendest, as I haf herde telle.
> Forthi an aunter in erde I attle to schawe,
> That a selly in sight summe men hit holden,
> And an outtrage awenture of Arthurez wonderez.

61

If ye wyl lysten this laye bot on littel quile,
I schal telle hit as-tit, as I in toun herde,
   with tonge,
  As hit is stad and stoken
  In stori stif and stronge,
  With lel letteres loken,
  In londe so hatz ben longe.   (I. 20-36)[10]

The tone of the first few lines is epic in the most monumental
sense of the word.[11] We have reference to a Britain founded by
a mighty warrior, followed by "baret that lofden"; it is the
England we learn of from Old English epic. But what distin-
guishes this island from other lands? Not so much its bold
warriors and great cities as the fact that "Mo ferlyes" have
happened here than anywhere else. It is at this point that the
poet first mentions Arthur. In the first half of this stanza, as
in the first stanza of the poem, we are led to expect great battles
and world-historical events. But in the second half of the stanza
we learn that the story will be of "aunter" and "selly." We
must revise our expectations to allow for surprise and wonder.

Indeed, we must revise our expectations everywhere through-
out this poem, and such reversed dialectic is at the heart of the
poet's manipulation of the audience. As the subject of the poem
moves from "seeges" to "ferlyes," the poet's voice becomes
increasingly skeptical and distant. The first stanza is stirring
and magnificent, as if the narrator were a primeval epic poet
speaking as the collective memory of his race. But as soon as
the true subject of the poem is admitted, the voice begins to
qualify, to make clear its own mnemonic devices and sources,
indeed, to shift the blame in a rather sophisticated manner from
the poet to his sources, from the absolute of history to the
relative of fiction: "as I in toun herde," "summe men hit hol-
den," "as I haf herde telle."

The second stanza, then, is constructed of an epic statement,
a transition that admits of wonder, followed by a revision that
states that indeed the theme *is* wonder. In addition, however,
the stanza itself forms a transition between the epic statement

of the first stanza and the outright romance setting of the rest of the fitt, particularly the holiday spirit in stanzas three and four. It is one thing to move from the mention of epic adventure to that of romance "aventure," but quite another to shift abruptly to games and celebration. Eventually, of course, we learn more in this poem about the profound nature of holidays and games.[12] But in the beginning the transitional stanza is important. The third stanza has another quality about it that sets it apart. It would be a fine stanza with which to end a romance. Here it begins a romance. The symmetrical structure of *Sir Gawain and the Green Knight* allows the poem also to end with such a scene, but there the gaiety of the court is abbreviated. Of course, analogues can be found for most of the elements in these opening stanzas. It is not unusual for alliterative poems to refer to a heroic historical tradition. What is worth noting here is the marked shift in tone within the first three stanzas, a shift that involves a distinctly different conception of human action.

These opening stanzas also show how many ways men have of organizing the past. The epic history of the first stanza impresses us with political and military events and how they bear upon our "own" time. The second stanza emphasizes mythic events, which are recalled when we tell them, and which seem to lack a causal link. The third stanza plunges us into a specific moment, a holiday, which is a way of renewing and, for a moment, redeeming one version of human time. The nature of holidays is such that the necessities of everyday life—food, clothing, meeting, and talking—become ritualized into feasts, costumes, parties, and speeches, and hence assume an importance that exceeds their function. What is dismaying about the society portrayed here is that they seem to live every day as a holiday.

Although the third stanza contains nothing but praise for Arthur's court, the holiday celebration is a change in status from the epic qualities that announce the poem. The court stands out in brilliance, but also with glare. We have yet to see why the court should deserve such laud. Arthur resembles, as Benson has said of Gawain himself, Chaucer's Squire rather than Chaucer's Knight, and the opening here in some ways resembles *The Squire's Tale*.[13] In addition, we have "reuel oryght and rechles merthes," "caroles," and "daunsyng." However all that may be, the poet is careful to insist that this is a bold *comitatus*, "So hardy a here on hille." But he goes on to describe Arthur's courtiers in terms of their social graces, not their military accomplishments. A good knight must have both credentials, but we see only one and must be told the other.

That social graces are emphasized is noteworthy too, for the language of the poem itself begins at times to sound like *vers de société*. Such witty and elegant discourse is part of courtly narrative. Chrétien had it; Chaucer uses it once in a while, too. When contained in such a majestic verse form and preceded not long before by epic trumpets, however, it begins to sound the slightest bit like chatter. The detailed description of clothing, too, sounds something like commentary in a fashion show, and the chronicling of the pageant of this feast, with its Froissart-like presence of the narrator, is not too different from accounts of opening night at the opera:[14] "There gode Gawan watz graythed Gwenore bisyde, / And Agrauayn a la dure mayn on that other syde sittes, / Bothe the kynges sistersunes and ful siker knightes." There is much of this observation for its own sake, and the catalogue grows increasingly detailed, down to the food, the service, the table service, indeed, the very embroidery of the tablecloth. But in the very next stanza the Green Knight appears.

The confrontation that ensues has been described as a duel between civilization and nature, or the human and the superhuman.[15] I am not entirely certain that the *Gawain*-poet will allow us to rest on such certainty and clear contrast. It is possible, I think, to overemphasize the churlishness of the Green Knight's behavior or to miss the note of irony in that scene in Bercilak's castle where Gawain is welcomed as a paragon of manners. Indeed, an audience impressed with ritual and formality would be likely to find Camelot a more suitably "aristocratic" setting. Bercilak's castle might be too comfortable to be true, too redolent of bourgeois *gemütlichkeit*. But this is to take seriously what is offered in the poem with sly good humor, and it precludes an even more interesting possibility for reading the poem in social terms: it is always the newly arrived member of any elect group who sets rigid standards of behavior and who pays most attention to often ritualistic manners. Those who have inherited a tradition are more likely to be at ease with it and to accept such concerns without obsession. The "nwe age" of Arthur's reign and the modish manners of his court may not be satiric comments on an overly self-conscious group; the comfort of Bercilak's castle may not indicate an older, more secure order; but at least such considerations blur, as the poet would wish, a black-and-white vision of social or natural order.

Gawain's sense that he is fighting for the court as a larger society, that he is about to face doom, is something of a feint, taking too seriously an inverted historical role. The real danger is the danger of romance—individual, timeless, ethical—and it is expressed not in physical action, but in the language games that go on between Gawain and the lady. We are prepared to face, as the hero is, the adventure that is suggested by the epic quality of alliterative verse, by the "form," but the heart of the hero's trial lies in the complicated romance plot of manners and morals, the "content." In a curious way these expectations of the reader are played off against each other—one bold, old, clearly defined, the other new, arch, sophisticated, foreign and cunning—which surprises us when we relax, or relaxes us in order to surprise.

The poet's rhetorical strategy, then, seems to follow a definite pattern. We are given a passage that suggests a certain system of values. Then we have a transition, perhaps as brief as a line, that warns of a change. After this, we are given another passage, which causes us to revise the first statement. Lest we question too much, however, the narrator generally corrects us. His method seems to be to suggest how a concrete situation can also be ambiguous and throw the audience off balance, forcing us to search for some frame of reference to orient ourselves, which he graciously provides.

The most concentrated description of action in *Sir Gawain*

65

and the Green Knight is one that we are likely to pass over
quickly in reading. I quote the entire stanza:

> Mony klyf he ouerclambe in contrayez straunge,
> Fer floten fro his frendez fremedly he rydez.
> At vche warthe other water ther the wyghe passed
> He fonde a foo hym byfore, bot ferly hit were,
> And that so foule and so felle that feght hym byhode.
> So mony meruayl bi mount ther the mon fyndez,
> Hit were to tore for to telle of the tenthe dole.
> Sumwhyle wyth wormez he werrez, and with wolues
>   als,
> Sumwhyle wyth wodwos, that woned in the knarrez,
> Bothe wyth bullez and berez, and borez otherquyle,
> And etaynez, that hym anelede of the heghe felle;
> Nade he ben dughty and dryghe, and Dryghten had
>   serued,
> Douteles he hade ben ded and dreped ful ofte.
> For werre wrathed hym not so much that wynter nas
>   wors,
> When the colde cler water fro the cloudez schadde,
> And fres er hit falle myght to the fale erthe;
> Ner slayn wyth the slete he sleped in his yrnes
> Mo nyghtez then innoghe in naked rokkez,
> Ther as claterande fro the crest the colde borne rennez,
> And henged heghe ouer his hede in hard iisse-ikkles.
> Thus in peryl and payne and plytes ful harde
> Bi contray caryez this knyght, tyl Krystmasse euen,
>   al one;
>   The knyght wel that tyde
>   To Mary made his mone,
>   That ho hym red to ryde
>   And wysse hym to sum wone.   (II. 713-739)

The passage has been praised for both its nature description and
psychological acuity. More remarkable, however, is that we
have in encapsulated form the various sorts of adventures that
the romance knight often encounters in the plot of an entire

narrative. Here they are reduced to a stanza. The martial prowess of the chivalric hero, however much it may be expended on fantastic deeds, is abbreviated, as if to say that this is not the end-all and be-all of human existence and certainly not its most memorable task. The lengthy ritual arming of Gawain has preceded this, and it has taken him far longer to arm himself than to carry out the tasks for which he is armed, at least in terms of our experience of the narrative.[16]

Again we note that the stanza divides into two distinct units, separated by the period at line 725 and hinged upon the sentence which that period ends. The first half concerns supernatural, "romance" adventure—dragons and giants and wild men—and a few natural bulls and bears. The second half describes only the ravages of the "contrayez straunge," a wasteland where isolation and not confrontation is the horror. Indeed, the reference to Gawain's virtue, "dughty and dryghe," and his service to God, though it refers to the fighting too, forms a transition to the description of winter, and the wasteland, as if to say that the protection of God is needed even more to get through this latter ordeal.

This passage is also responsible for recording what happens from the time of Gawain's departure from Camelot on All Saint's Day to his arrival at Bercilak's castle. Although the description is formal in style, the representation of time's passing is imprecise: "Somewhyle . . . Somewhyle."[17] Gawain's knowledge of a fate he must face at the end of a year allows the passing of that year to be represented, almost psychologically, as frittered away. The audience's experience of time is also manipulated in that as the end of the year approaches, suspense increases and the narrative slows down, whirling through the seasons until a slow November and December; the last three days seem longest of all. The brief description of these dangers— the threat of a supernatural confrontation in the first half, of an existential isolation in the second half—inform our understanding of the rest of the story, for the meeting with the Green Knight offers not only parts of both dangers but also a *tertium quid*. The passage also disarms us, for we are not prepared for

67

the other test in the castle of Bercilak, which is different from these adventures in the wilderness where the dangers are obvious.

The most interesting of these stanzaic divisions points up a contradiction in the hero, and by extension, in the members of his audience who aspire to his perfection. The language of Gawain is, throughout, the language of the chivalric hero. The court of Bercilak even hopes to learn something of the language of love from him. Finally, however, Bercilak unravels for Gawain all the ramifications of the details of the plot, some of which no doubt seemed as insignificant to Gawain as to us. This time Gawain's answer seems curiously inappropriate, defensive. His speech begins with the courteous farewell of the perfect courtier, as if nothing had happened:

> "Nay, for sothe," quoth the segge, and sesed hys helme,
> And hatz hit of hendely, and the hathel thonkkez,
> "I haf soiorned sadly; sele yow bytyde,
> And he yelde hit yow yare that yarkkez al menskes!"
>
> (IV. 2407-2410)

But suddenly, with only a pause for breath, the stanza that contains this speech breaks almost in perfect half, with the first half (the above lines) courtly and chivalric, and the second half rude, immoderate, misogynist. The middle sentence is the hinge, gradually shading into a markedly different sort of discourse:

> "And comaundez me to that cortays, your comlych fere,
> Both that on and that other, myn honored ladyez,
> That thus hor knyght wyth hor kest han koyntly bigyled.
> Bot hit is no ferly thagh a fole madde,
> And thurgh wyles of wymmen be wonen to sorghe,
> For so watz Adam in erde with one bygyled,
> And Salamon with fele sere, and Samson eftsonez—
> Dalyda dalt hym hys wyrde—and Dauyth therafter
> Watz blended with Barsabe, that much bale tholed.
> Now these were wrathed wyth her wyles, hit were a wynne
>   huge

To luf hom wel, and leue hem not, a leude that couthe.
For thes wer forne the freest, that folghed alle the sele
Exellently of alle thyse other, vnder heuenryche
    that mused;
And alle thay were biwyled
With wymmen that thay vsed.
Thagh I be now bigyled,
Me think me burde be excused."   (IV. 2411-2428)

Whatever we make of this extraordinary and comic speech, the first thing we note about it is that it begins with the language of the courtier and ends with the language of the cleric. It is as if the strain of chivalric behavior were too much to bear; the slightest note of hysteria creeps into the speech. The speech is a momentary lapse, no doubt, but it completes the irony of Gawain's language journey, from the language of the epic hero to that of the romance hero to that of the biblical tragic hero. One wonders if Gawain must escape from the court to the cloister to right the score of sexual balances upset in the bedroom scenes. He achieves a synthesis between these worlds in the next stanza, wearing the courtly trophy as an act of penance. In addition, the list of problematic couples in the stanza quoted above forms a revised historical background for the poem, replacing the chronicle of Troy, Greece, Rome, and Britain early in the poem. History becomes not the tragedy of cities, but the tragedy of sex. One wonders too if the list of Old Testament characters is meant to suggest to us a certain type of woman in a world not yet saved: Eve, Sheba, Delilah, Bathsheba. Are we meant to rethink the history of the prologue and think not only of Troy but of Helen and so on? However that may be, the message is clear: it is far better to be Mary's knight, but we are condemned also to be Delilah's.

The last stanza of the poem also breaks in two, but there the movement from large to small is reversed. Gawain speaks to the court in a tone of voice that is not merely modest but genuinely contrite. The passage moves to the general from the personal by means of a vaguely proverbial expression:

For mon may hyden his harme, bot vnhap ne may hit,
For ther hit onez is tachched twynne wil hit neuer.
(IV. 2511-2512)

The rest of the passage, which fades us out of the poem's world, records an action that is more courtly than clerical. Amid general laughter, Arthur's court responds to Gawain by all promising to wear the green girdle, but as a symbol of honor rather than of penance. The language of the stanza then picks up a stirring quality. We are reminded of the "best bok of romaunce" and are suddenly distanced from the poem's frame to Arthur's day, and thence to Brutus' day. It finally ends, however, with a blessing that transcends these moments. The poet recalls another action at once penitential and heroic, though its suffering and wounding was more profound than Gawain's and its "blysse" more profound than the laughter of the court.

BY UNBALANCING the reader's response to certain passages, the poem calls into question some of its own techniques as well as the reader's perception. Perhaps it is safer to say that certain images comment ironically on the ways in which the characters and the reader make sense of the events that occur in the story. For instance, the poem critically examines the limits of vision, language and rules, all of which play an essential part in the story, and which play an essential part in telling the story.

In a poem that depends for much of its effect upon visual, ecphrastic rhetoric and the pictorialization of each detail, the narrator's obsession with "eyes" is especially notable.[18] In the description of Guenevere the last detail is her "yghen gray" (I. 82), traditional in a courtly heroine. The Green Knight himself approaches the court: "Gladly I wolde / Se that segg in syght . . .' / To knyghtez he kest his yghe, / and reled hym vp and doun" (I. 225-229). Later, the eyelids of Gawain will be mentioned again and again, for we often see him waking out of a comfortable sleep, both when the lady enters his bedchamber and when, on the last morning, he wakes to face his fate.

Eyes recur throughout the poem, each time revealing something about their owner: the courtly portraiture of Guenevere who never says a word in the poem, the droll challenge of the Green Knight as he rolls his eyes, the collective stupefaction of the court who literally cannot believe their eyes, the wary and wakeful eyes of Gawain who uneasily opens his eyes and is almost ready to close them again. The narrator's own technique occasionally involves a pattern of focusing his scene on smaller and smaller details, sometimes dwelling upon the eyes of characters, then suddenly cutting to a larger scene, as if reflecting what those eyes see. The audience too reads the poem with its eyes, even if it is read to them, for its appreciation of the poem requires a keen imaginative recreation of color and movement. Yet readers, as well as the hero, can have eyes and still not see significant clues, such as the physical resemblance of Bercilak to the Green Knight, or the coincidental color of the girdle.

Critics have called attention to the fact that the *Gawain*-poet suggests size, distance, and perspective by means of juxtaposition. What I would add here is that such a contrast of details and perspectives gives the reader a sense of fragmentation, a slight, dreamlike lag between stimulus and response. The narrator beguiles us with the beauty of detail then suddenly draws back (or vice-versa), and we feel the shock. In a scene such as the entry of Bercilak into Camelot, we have been lulled into a sense of verisimilitude when we are suddenly presented with the Green Knight. Like the court, we cannot believe our eyes. Bercilak's castle itself springs up like a conjurer's illusion. A nagging distrust of vision, ironic in a poem that depends so strongly on pictorialization, is always in the background.

Similarly, the role of language, equally crucial in a poem of such obvious verbal brilliance, is also mildly questioned. I have already commented on the narrator's qualification of his source in the opening, when he tells us that he has himself heard this story "in toune." The fiction of oral transmission is carried through the poem until the end, where his authority becomes "the best boke of romaunce." In addition, the poem uses court conversation, which at best can be a vehicle of power, memory,

71

and fame, at worst, slander and gossip. Later Gawain is welcomed at the castle so that the guests might learn of "luf-talkyng." His test in the castle will be as much verbal as anything else. His characteristic defense will be language, with which he will parry the lady's conversational gambit, and thus stall for time, while Bercilak, in a characteristic burst of activity, is out hunting. Such ironies are pointed out by the Green Knight himself: "Now is the reuel and the renoun of the Rounde Table / Ouerwalt wyth a worde of on wyghes speche" (I. 313-314). Although the Green Knight sarcastically propounds the power of speech, it is precisely the necessity for all this speech that forestalls action.

Gawain, after Arthur answers the Green Knight, eventually responds to the Green Knight's challenge, but he can hardly leave the table without the manners and language of courtly society obtruding, and he makes an admirable but perhaps too wordy speech:

> 'Wolde ye, worthilych lorde,' quoth Wawan to the kyng,
> 'Bid me boghe fro this benche, and stonde by yow there,
> That I wythoute vylanye mygh voyde this table,
> And that my legge lady lyked not ille,
> I wolde com to your counseyl bifore your cort ryche.
> For me think hit not semly, as hit is soth knawen,
> Ther such an askyng is heuened so hyghe in your sale,
> Thagh ye yourself be talenttyf, to take hit to youseluen,
> Whil mony so bolde yow aboute bench sytten,
> That vnder heuen I hope non hagherer of wylle,
> Ne better bodyes on bent ther baret is rered.
> I am the wakkest, I wot, and of wyt feblest,
> And lest lur of my lyf, quo laytes the sothe—
> Bot for as much as ye ar myn em I am only to prayse,
> No bounté bot your blod I in my bodé knowe;
> And sythen this note is so nys that noght hit yow falles,
> And I haue frayned hit at yow fyrst, foldez hit to me;
> And if I carp not comlyly, let alle this cort rych bout blame.'
>
> (I. 343-361)

Nearly all the moral issues of the poem are hinted at here in ways that will double back on Gawain, and cause his final speech to the court to be something of a retraction. The speech itself ends with a reference to his ability to "carp." It cannot be said of Gawain that he is all talk and no action; he is indeed possessed, as a good knight should be, of both. Here, though, the baggage of language becomes cumbersome.

The most common form of conversation we find in the poem, as one would expect from a quest form, is a question. After the beheading, Gawain asks the Green Knight who he is:

"Where schulde I wale the," quoth Gauan, "where is thy place?
I wot neuer where thou wonyes, bi hym that me wroght,
Ne I know not the, knyght, the cort ne thi name."
(I. 398-400)

The question, and the evasive answer, are significant, because although Gawain defines himself by his court and his name and seems to lose power in his own eyes by not being defined in such a way, the Green Knight seems to lose power by being given the simple name of Bercilak, who is in some way bound to Morgan le Fay, although I suppose it is a false response to feel sorry for him at the end. At any rate, Gawain's questions continue:

And ay he frayned, as he ferde, at frekez that he met,
If thay had herde any karp of a knyght grene,
In any grounde theraboute, of the grene chapel.
(II. 703-705)

But the answers are hard in coming, and Gawain's questions take a more general and metaphysical form:

"Quat schuld I wonde?
Of destinés derf and dere
What may mon do bot fonde?"
(II. 563-565)

Finally, when the lady implies that the real Gawain would never act like this, his question becomes truly plaintive: "Querfore?"

(III. 1294). The audience too is involved in a question, also with
a delayed answer, which the narrator phrases for us and for the
court: "What thenne?" (I. 462). The gap in time between ques-
tion and answer is of crucial importance, for as much as *Sir
Gawain and the Green Knight* is about various sorts of games,
it is also a waiting game, which, in a medieval eschatological
framework, is to say life itself. The arrangements of the first
fitt are in terms of time for the most part, and although the
Green Knight is vague about the location of the Green Chapel
(just ask, he says), he is quite specific about the time: exactly
a year from New Year's Day.

Just as games do, language and speaking have rules for con-
trolling them. Although this is obvious in the bedroom scenes,
it is also evident in the tradition that requires Arthur to invite
even this strange green guest to share their repast. But for a
moment there is silence. Do the rules have limits?

> Forthi for fantoum and fayryghe the folk there hit demed.
> Therefore to answare watz arghe mony athel freke,
> And al stouned at his steuen and stonstil seten
> In a swoghe sylence thurgh the sale riche;
> As al were slypped vpon slepe so slaked hor lotez
> in hyghe . . .   (I. 240-245)

Or is the fear of the Green Knight the fear of answering a
"fantoum"? No, instead, hierarchy is involved here:

> I deme hit not al for doute,
> Bot sum for cortaysye—
> Bot let hym that al schulde loute
> Cast vnto that wyghe.
>   (I. 246-249)

The court is waiting, we are told, for Arthur to speak. The order
that for every being finds a function and for every situation
finds a characteristic ceremony here falters for a second. And
in that faltering, the poet, ironically correcting a response that
we might not have had quite yet, finds a rule. In finding the
limits of his perfection, Gawain too is being forced to find his

74

order, identity, and potential. He will lapse momentarily and in that lapse find significance.

THE DELICATE BALANCE of the poem always threatens to fall apart, but the poem always returns safely from excursions into the seemingly inconsequential, into details so minute that to follow the poet's eye is to lose oneself in the trees, to be lost in a forest for which, until we finish the poem, we have no map. If in fact we stand back from *Sir Gawain and the Green Knight* and examine it as we would a map, its forceful symmetry is clear. At the beginning and the end we have the two contests, intrusions from another world. At the flanks, two courts, Arthur's and Bercilak's. In the center, the incredible polyphony between the hunt and the bedroom scenes. Even the architectural settings are parallel with each other, with the description of the castle after the second fitt and the description of the Green Chapel at the end of the poem. But between such places—now primitive, now civilized—runs the figure of Gawain, unconscious of the polarity or the analogy, as a reader is likely to be, until the very end.

Gawain's own point of view in fact reflects a morbid eschatology. Faced by the imminence of his own death, Gawain is blind both to smaller but more important crises and to intimations of salvation, which may undercut his tragic stoicism. For Gawain, the test at the Green Chapel will be a microcosm of the Judgment: "as God wyl me suffer / To dele on Nw Yerez day the dome of my wyrdes" (III. 1967-1968). But if Gawain insists on imposing a pattern of finality on the world, the Green Knight and all the forces of nature that seem to be part of his domain are all too willing to supply mirages of doom. The Green Knight returns again and again, now in this form, now in that, like the plot itself, for "A yere yernes ful yerne, and yeldez neuer lyke / The forme to the fynisment foldez ful selden" (II. 498-499). Gawain must learn that the test may come at any time and more likely than not will come from within.

This preoccupation with perception lies behind the poem's narrative style and its obsession with rendering the experience

75

of time and space. Renoir and others have compared the *Gawain*-poet's style to the cinema, and this does not seem to me merely a modern misconception.[19] The narrative is constructed of discrete "shots," each line describing a particular visual element. This narrative style makes a demand upon the reader perfectly consistent with the age's preoccupation with how man's vision can make sense of a world that no doubt looks very different from the perspective of its Creator. For us, each perspective can only be partial.

The architecture of the narrative is one thing, the experience of reading or listening quite another. The clues that should tie together the details of the plot are passed over by the reader, since he is accustomed to the mode of perception—discrete, spatial, imagistic—that the style demands. Such a contradiction reveals not only a consummate narrative skill but also a subtle tension between the voice of the poet and his assumed audience, for despite its wonderful success as an entertainment, the poem deals explicitly with profound moral issues. The poet seems to have taken seriously his audience's demand that they be both instructed and amused at once. There have been many studies of how the poem's meaning is revealed in the action or symbols. I have tried to show how it is created by the style.

The "history" of Arthur's court is given before the fact. The ethics and motivation of his knights are revealed all at once in the beginning of the story. Thus we know about the court in a historical perspective. But Bercilak simply appears. His associations are revealed after the fact. In each case, the background is ironic, for Arthurian propaganda does not prepare the audience for the peculiar action of the story, nor does Bercilak's thraldom to Morgan explain his part in the story.[20] Neither does the predominantly epic association and monumental scale of alliterative verse sufficiently prepare us for the poem's quality of subtle romance and the poet's skill with character and conversation. To this extent, *Sir Gawain and the Green Knight* is about what we can learn from precedent.

The style that dwells in incredible detail on the profusion of things that makes up Gawain's world also challenges our ability to comprehend it all. It requires an act of almost devotional intensity on the reader's part to distinguish between significant and gratuitous detail, between the shimmer of jewelry and the aura of sanctity. As in the real world, a fine line divides the perception of transcendence in all things and the hedonistic obsession with their surfaces. Such a style teases us with our own imperfection, for we cannot read the poem from the vantage of Gawain, who vacillates between naiveté and paranoia, or Bercilak, who enjoys his complicity in making the obvious devious and the devious obvious, without taking into account the perspective of the poet, who like Morgan le Fay, may, or may not, have intended it all.[21]

The reader's attention must choose between stirring panorama and significant clue; it must get lost in the manic proliferation of things that makes up the body of the narrative and be caught, as Gawain is, between the significant and the insignificant, the necessary and the contingent. The loving description of each detail, however much it parallels the love of detail in some contemporary visual arts, also creates almost a mystical, totemic aura around each thing. Meaning glows from each detail, for the *Gawain*-poet was writing for a civilization and a class that perceived all the elements of the natural world as symbols of a greater order, an audience to whom the representation of physical reality seemed now increasingly gratuitous and now increasingly metaphoric, pointing always to a meaning beyond itself. The poet's best scenes involve intrusions from another world, impositions upon an already constructed scene, like the entrance of the Green Knight. The action must stop to allow the intruder to be described, almost constructed, piece by piece, in minute detail. The sudden appearance of an unexpected and surreal alien form throws upon the scene we have already accepted an aura of the otherworldly so that nothing can be as it once was and all the elements of phenomenal reality are suddenly open to question. The task of the *Gawain*-poet is to redeem his audience, as he does his hero, from such abstraction and to reassert the worth of both human values and physical reality.[22]

At the end of the poem we have a scene very much like that at the beginning. The poem ends with the same lines it began with. In one way, of course, the poem reaffirms the values with which it began. In a more profound way, however, that affirmation is ironic and admiring at once, not unlike the Green Knight's attitude towards Gawain, for the late fourteenth-century audience, like the hero, has undergone a test of its own values, disguised as a diversionary experience, as was Gawain's temptation. At times, like Gawain, the audience is tempted to give up on those values, to wonder, like the court, if it is all worth it, but the poet returns, with grace, to allow the audience to hold its values. Yet now the audience, if the poem has been anything more than a diversion, holds such values more gingerly and with recognition of their limitations. The tone of the opening includes audience, hero, and poet as celebrants of the same social values. The echo of this note at the end of the poem is far less comforting or certain.

The tone of *Sir Gawain and the Green Knight* is finally comic, and it is fitting that the poet treats us with the same gentle irony that marks his treatment of his hero. I have tried to show how that irony can have serious moral and cultural ramifications. We are similarly engaged in the experience of another great late fourteenth-century poem, Chaucer's *Troilus and Criseyde*. As the next chapter attempts to prove, however, human desire and human perception are treated in Chaucer's narrative with a far sterner irony. Our own way of making sense of the poem, and of the mutable world itself, has implications from which we cannot so easily escape.

CHAPTER 3

Consciousness and Time in
Troilus and Criseyde

*T*hings change. This is one of the few commonplaces that remains unscathed by the action of Chaucer's *Troilus and Criseyde*. For the fact that things do change is at the heart of Chaucer's "tragedie." It is also central to any reader's experience of the poem, for mutability, besides being a theme in this story, is also what makes a plot go forward.[1] From the point of view of heaven this world can be perceived not as a narrative but as a vision, which is how Troilus sees it from the "holughnesse of the eighthe spere."[2] But we are condemned to read the poem as a consecutive narrative. That such immersion in the narrative is discontinuous and subject to reconsideration at the end of the poem is neither a flaw in the poem's unity nor evidence of a forgotten aesthetic.[3] Rather, the "moral" of *Troilus and Criseyde* is experienced in the reading of the poem.[4]

The subject of this chapter, then, is the seduction and betrayal of the reader of *Troilus and Criseyde*. The gist of the best recent criticism of the poem has been to show how the narrator, the hero, and the philosophical background of the poem all change before our very eyes. My topic is how the audience is changed. In a sense, my approach has been to turn upside down the pyramid that critics have constructed between fiction, narrator, and reader. Earlier criticism, interested in the psychology of the characters, dealt with the story.[5] Criticism of the fifties and sixties, interested in mediation and formalism, put the narrator on top.[6] Here I am concerned with the influence of these two points on the third point, the reader.[7] Chaucer does, I hope to

79

prove, manipulate his reader as the narrative progresses, almost as if the reader too were a character.

At first the opening scenes communicate worldly elegance and the "courtliness" of courtly love: detached, arch, sophisticated, and if serious, serious in a mannered way. What happens in the course of the poem, however, is that this way of perceiving the action (and ourselves) is revised. The notion of the audience as "lovers" with which the poem's opening embraces us contrasts with the divine force of the love to which the poem finally dedicates itself. These images of earthly life, which the opening underscores, are redeemed at the end of the poem as problematic concepts rather than as elegant forms that blind us to the transience of the earthly world.

This is not to say that Chaucer does not warn us of the seriousness of his story. It is precisely the fact that he warns but does not convince us that is the central fact of the narrator's opening address. We are told what the story will be and how the movement of the plot will go:

> The double sorwe of Troilus to tellen,
> That was the kyng Priamus sone of Troye,
> In lovynge, how his aventures fellen
> Fro wo to wele, and after out of joie.
>
> (I. 1-4)

The poet calls to the goddess of torment and in good classical fashion asks her to help him assume a suitable decorum:

> For wel sit it, the sothe for to Seyne
> A woful wight to han a drery feere,
> And to a sorwful tale, a sory chere.
>
> (I. 12-14)

There is nothing here to suggest that the story will be a happy one. The narrator knowing the end, warns of its effect. But in a way he is wasting his breath, for empathy is something the audience must learn for itself. Indeed, the tone of the following stanzas suggest that the narrator too will go through the experience again, which may account for his own pain later.

80

This depth of meaning is lost on audiences or readers who, as "loveres, that bathen in gladnesse," may not be entirely capable of appreciating the force of the warning, for given the limits of an understanding bound by time and space, and communication by a narrative fiction, this wisdom is not something that can simply be stated. We must exercise our linear understanding of history in order to understand, paradoxically, the limits of that understanding. We are not only young lovers who are being instructed by a figure who combines the archness of Ovid, the obtuseness of Andreas, the manipulations of Pandarus himself; we also experience the extremes of love, in the form of our reactions to the story itself. We are forced to become participants as well as voyeurs.

In some French romances and their English redactions a certain relationship between audience, characters, and narrators exists. There the narrator, a clerk, perhaps older and wiser, tells a sophisticated audience the story of naive young lovers. The result is a dominant tone of condescension and amusement, a feeling that things will turn out all right because problems are not nearly as serious as the young lovers think. The audience, in these earlier romances, feels a note of nostalgia, of vicarious participation in the simplicities of an adolescent vision of life. This may well be the expectation of the reader of the *Troilus*, at least at first, and the narrator heartily fulfills that expectation. But this satisfaction does not last long. The force of felt experience and the complexity of the characters exceed the conventional framework of romance and threaten the relative safety of the reader.

That Calkas, Criseyde's father, knows Troy will be destroyed and flees to the Greeks is of great significance for the narrative:

> A gret devyn, that clepid was Calkas,
> That in science so expert was that he
> Knew wel that Troie sholde destroied be,
> By answere of his god, that highte thus,
> Daun Phebus or Appollo Delphicus.
>
> (I. 66-70)

Interestingly, we do not know precisely of how much significance Calkas' knowledge will be until the fourth book. We are in some ways bound by the time and space of the narrative, as Calkas and Chaucer are not. Much has been made of Calkas' knowledge in regard to the ideology of predestination expounded at times in the poem. But Calkas' foreknowledge is, as Bloomfield has pointed out, responsible for causing the tragedy at one level.[8] To the extent that the narrator is privy to knowledge of what is to come, he is "guilty" of causing us to share in the pain of the tragedy. Perhaps that is why he gets more and more defensive. However that may be, we too know that Troy will be destroyed, and we know that Troilus' and Criseyde's love will end unhappily. But there are different sorts of knowledge as there are different sorts of love. It is one thing to know that the story will end unhappily, but quite another to feel the woe. Higher beings may well be able to know and to feel at the same time. That may be what the ending attempts to achieve in us. What the narrative does, however, is show us that we can feel and understand the reality of an experience only by perceiving it temporally, even though the narrative intrusions warn us of what is to come and even though we know that temporal perception is limited and imperfect.

This double consciousness is the double sorrow of the reader. The sorrow lies in responding to the story with complete empathy and at the same time recognizing the inevitability of the vision with which the poem ends. It is possible finally to see the ways in which human and divine love are related, but it is not an easy task. Reading or listening becomes a "sorrow," and we are subject, with Troilus, to both a painful education and a more painful reeducation, until we, too, are promoted to the grade of heaven from which he finally sees the world, and to a place above that station too, which one can only reach by means of grace. The argument that the reader must choose one sorrow or the other, that the palinode is detachable or the narrative is ironic, would minimize our plight.[9] But we are to be allowed no such solace.

The dance of the narrative itself, the movements of this part of the poem, still a very strange "Trojan" scene, are highly formalized.[10] There is no denying Criseyde's vulnerability or Hector's noble pity, but the scene of supplication is a tableau:

> On knees she fil beforn Ector adown
> With pitous vois and tendrely wepynge,
> His mercy bad, hirselven excusynge.
>
> (I. 110-112)

We know later that the "hirselven excusynge" is a characteristic of Criseyde's personality, but for now, it is all part of the formal scene. If I suggest that such a scene is like some late medieval paintings of kneeling and forgiving figures, it is less to imply indebtedness than to point out the detached, iconlike formality of the poses, framed off from us. Characters in these early scenes are described in terms of strategic positions, relative to each other, and such positions are usually pregnant with meaning. Criseyde is described thus:

> And yet she stood ful lowe and stille allone,
> Byhynden other folk, in litel brede,
> And neigh the dore.
>
> (I. 178-180)

Troilus moves:

> as he was wont to gide
> His yonge knyghtes, lad hem up and down
> In thilke large temple on every side,
> Byholding ay the ladies of the town . . .
>
> (I. 183-186)

Chaucer rarely indulges in much background description, but his *mis en scene* can suggest an almost Jamesian interconnection of characters.[11]

At such an early point in the narrative the audience is not conscious of its own participation in the dance. Our suggested pose is a formal pose, unlike the emotional plea of the narrator. Such formality allows us an aloof reserve, for we have no way of measuring the reality of the narrator's grief. We watch the dance from a distance. And because of this distance we are conscious only in retrospect of the weight of the narrator's exclamation:

> O blynde world, O blynde entencioun!
> How often falleth al the effect contraire
> Of surquidrie and foul presumpcioun;
> For kaught is proud, and kaught is debonaire.
> This Troilus is clomben on the staire,
> And litel weneth that he moot descenden;
> But alday faileth thing that fooles wenden.
>
> (I. 211-217)

In terms of the reader's involvement in the story at this point, such a plea is likely to sound out of place, a bit hysterical. It is a forewarning, but a warning that only in retrospect justifies its seriousness. Indeed, the narrator, as if conscious of this, switches to the lively, earthy image of "Bayard," thus putting us at ease by turning to a less elevated style. Chaucer dresses an image with an aristocratic literary heritage in a popular color.[12] We can be both sympathetic and amused again.

Troilus is scornful of the power of love but is doomed to bend to it, even "though he a worthy kynges sone were," which should warn the audience, who are also lovers, to take this story more seriously, since it is about love and its powers:

> Forthy ensample taketh of this man,
> Ye wise, proude, and worthi folkes alle,
> To scornen Love, which that so soone kan
> The fredom of youre hertes to hym thralle;
> For evere it was, and evere it shall byfalle,
> That Love is he that alle thing may bynde,
> For may no man fordon the lawe of kynde.
>
> (I. 232-238)

Again we are not inclined to take such warnings very seriously at this point. Only by following the story, which for a reader is the "lawe of kynde" of fiction, can we understand the significance of a higher law that is beyond the limits of fiction.

84

But we cannot avoid either law, and our limited understanding reaches the latter only by way of the former. In addition, the tone of the passage implies that our detached perspective is doomed, perhaps by the very amusement that lets us smile at this warning of the narrator.

The entrance of Pandarus further complicates our response, and as a number of critics have suggested, he becomes the stage manager of the action within the poem, at least in the second and third books, just as the narrator manages the action between story and audience.[13] Pandarus can be subtle after his fashion, but his typical speech consists of stating in cruder terms what the reader has either already been told or has already suspected. His is a mentality that permits action but leaves a great deal out. More to the point, however, is his function:

> And went his wey, thenkyng on this matere,
> And how he best myghte hire biseche of grace,
> And fynde a tyme therto, and a place.
>
> (I. 1062-1064)

Like the function of narrative on its most literal level, Pandarus seeks the appropriate time and the appropriate place. The reader too follows the action in this way, though like Troilus, he sees in this action a significance that can partially transcend a "tyme" and a "place." But we must begin, as Pandarus does, with the literal level of fiction, as with that of love. Our fascination at this point with Pandarus' exuberance and "realism" is a sign of our mutable imagination. Indeed, a modern reader might take him to be the most sensible character. But to take him that way is to read only part of the poem. He takes us on part of our journey, but he is also a guide who must be discarded at a certain level of consciousness if we are to travel any further. We must pay attention to the facts of time and place in order to see beyond them. For the moment the reader's mind is on the machinations that the narrator and Pandarus are busy with. The introduction of Pandarus into the poem at this point, with his wit, his "experience," the efficiency with which one not in love may act, provides a way for the reader to join in the dance.

His entrance is a way of breaking down our distance from the action, for he speaks, however comically and on occasion ludicrously, for a detached, friendly interest, halfway between sympathy and gossip. But what one gains in this ally, one must pay for by giving up a sense of courtly elegance.

A preoccupation with time and suspense is expressed in a profoundly different way by Troilus: "But, Lord, how shal I doon? How shal I lyven?" (II. 981). Time is the enemy of lovers—too long before they are together, too short once they are. Of course, such waiting is conditioned by the fact that for the reader fiction is a way of passing time. Time will, however, also bring about the sad end as well as the time-transcending epilogue. There is indeed a moral here, for Troilus' specific question becomes our general and moral question. Such a meaning does not exist at this point in the narrative, but in the *Troilus*, as Baldwin has shown in *The Canterbury Tales*, there is a progression from specific, mundane meanings to a more general, metaphysical temporal significance.[14]

It is clear by the end of the first book that we are not going to be allowed the luxury of distance reserved for the audiences of love allegories and chivalric romances. The patronizing, slightly parental relationship of audience to characters in sentimental love romances will not be possible either. Indeed, with both Chaucer as narrator and Pandarus constantly interpreting the action for us, it becomes necessary for the reader to sneak behind both mediators to understand the hero and heroine. Emphasis on the narrator and fascination with Pandarus as a character have made us pay attention to how these two mediate the action. But the audience or reader is also faced with the problem of such commentary obfuscating the action, and all that distance paradoxically forces us to interpret the action "directly," if only out of exasperation.

The dismissal of the static pose that the audience took towards the action in the first book are part of the object of the invocation to the second book. Its subject is history, but it is a history that encompasses us. Ostensibly, it distances us from the action, blocks us off from a story that happened in the past, but it also points out that the forces that move the plot are the forces that move us, and not just in terms of the flattering inclusion of us as "loveres" in the opening of the first book. There the Trojan War, which is the setting for the story, was an event that took place in the past, which we could listen to safely and study from a sympathetically interested distance. But the historiography that opens Book II involves audience, work, and author as well as characters. That the skies are clearing and the sea calming is part of the illusion and only temporary, something we should remember about history, too. The allegorical figures who fill the borders of the narrative—Clio, Fortuna, the Furies, even Venus—seem to be working towards similar goals, even if they have such different faces. Any reader is liable to feel more comfortable about a section inspired by Clio than one guided by the Furies, partly because we imagine that Clio would be more objective and allow some distance from the emotions of the narrative. But that too is a mistake. Like language, and hence like the medium of this narrative, we are subject to the same forces of change as the protagonists, and the scholarliness with which this fact is expressed is part of the trap. There is less gnashing of teeth and regret in this invocation than in that to Book I, so we are pacified. Such distance may well be what a reader wishes at this point. Paradoxically, that calm, like the eye of a hurricane, is a sign that the reader has been drawn into this history, which has ceased to be objective and far away. In reemphasizing the historicity of the action in this fashion, the invocation actually proclaims its immediate relevance. We are told that all this is strange and remote, but the scenes that follow between Pandarus and Criseyde are brilliantly "present," unlike the more exotic opening of the first book. Similarly, the act of reading is put into perspective, for we meet Criseyde listening to a story of siege, as we are, and though the shock of recognition is a distancing device; at the same time, it lets us know this world is not so very different from a fourteenth-century world.

As we begin to reconsider our response towards the story, the narrator suggests a subtle shift in the audience's pose. The voice at the beginning of the first book was not only a poet but a "chaplain" of love, advising young lovers; and the ensuing scenes took place in a temple. The voice at the beginning of the second book begins to sound a bit like a historian lecturing on a particular theory of history. Furthermore, the tone-setting scene that opens the second book is not religious but literary-historical in nature. Criseyde and her maidens are reading from the "geste of the siege of Thebes." We are to be not only courtly lovers but seekers after a truth that still affects us. The pose of the narrator in the first book as a preacher was reflected in the frontispiece to one of the manuscripts of the *Troilus*, which shows Chaucer reading as from a pulpit. But the court of love is not the implied scene in the opening to the second book. We are now in a scriptorium, overlooking old manuscripts; we are humanists rather than courtiers. Although we gain in what we consider objectivity, we lose the gay self-protective sophistication of the courtier. Suddenly we are made to feel more like Chaucer's Clerk than Chaucer's Squire.

In the first book the encounters between the figures seemed random. Their movements, although stylized, were spontaneous, accidental, brought up short only by confrontation with something more moving than they had expected. Criseyde stands at the side of the temple. Troilus is coincidentally walking up and down the aisles. The God of Love, annoyed, looks down. Troilus, his eyes circling the temple, sees Criseyde by "chance." Later a friend calls upon the grieved young man. Now we are certainly conscious that these encounters are contrived by the author. Indeed, he is bound to describe their actions from a source that predetermines them. We are conscious enough too that these meetings, between Troilus and Criseyde, like those of Romeo and Juliet and Tristan and Iseult, are in some way fated. But the movements of the characters are made to seem as if they were accidental.

Now in the second book all the various movements, primarily due to the intercession of Pandarus, strike us as directed towards the specific goal of the lovers' meeting. This teleology is part of our involvement at this point not only in the spirit but in the mechanics of the story. We know Pandarus is about to call on Criseyde, so his meeting with her is described in a brief, stage-direction-like interchange:

> Whan he was come unto his neces place,
> "Wher is my lady?" to hire folk quod he;
> And they hym tolde, and he forth in gan pace,
> And fond two othere ladys sete, and she.
>
> (II. 78-81)

As critics have noted, Pandarus and the lovers expend an enormous amount of ingenuity and art to bring about what has already been ordained by fate. The reader begins to see a design in all these manipulations; the plan has been in evidence everywhere, like the design of providence, but it is only a certain perspective that uncovers it. Since our imaginations are capable only of temporary and partial perspectives, we see one part of the pattern now, one later; and we must depend on our memory, and that of the narrator, to free us from such illusion. The second book is no more choreographed than the first. It is just that we have joined the dance and are moving along with what we observe.

The narrator often mirrors the tactics of Pandarus and assumes his tone of voice. As the second book ends, he repeats Pandarus' poetics:

> But fle we now prolixitee best is,
> For love of God, and lat us faste go
> Right to th'effect, withouten tales mo,
> Whi al this folk assembled in this place . . .
>
> (II. 1564-1567)

The narrator begins here to remind us more and more of the details of time and space, to suggest perhaps that as static as the characters may seem, things are rushing to a head: "What shold I lenger in this tale tarien?" In the public scenes, when the important people of Troy are assembled, we are made acutely conscious of the historical recreation on the part of the poet and hence of the pastness of the action, but also of the passing of narrative time itself. Alone—in the conversations of Pandarus and Criseyde, in the love scenes of Troilus and Criseyde, in the emotional exaggeration and humor of Troilus' and Pandarus' scenes—we observe the characters as people; we are less conscious of the profound sweep of narrative time and history. The time-scheme of these private scenes is predicted on the passing of a day or an evening that might part these friends from each other. There is a sense, then, in which the reader is made to partake of Troilus' error, to imagine that mundane events could somehow be made impervious to mutability.

So as the second book ends, there are hints that the stance of the audience as objective, historical truth-seekers is about to be changed again, for this stance will also prove inadequate to the material at hand. A synthesis of the audience's poses is being effected:

> But now to yow, ye loveres that ben here,
> Was Troilus nought in a kankedort,
> That lay and myghte whisprynge of hem here,
> And thoughte, "O Lord, right now renneth my sort
> Fully to deye, or han anon comfort!"
> And was the firste tyme he shulde hire preye
> Of love; O myghty God, what shal he seye?
>
> (II. 1751-1757)

The audience becomes again "ye loveres." The public scene we see before us suggests the feudal structure of Troy, as well as the real historical forces acting upon its values, for later all these oaths will have no real meaning, changed, as words are changed, by the circumstances of time. Yet the question with which the book ends, in a form of suspense for the hero, is a question of language and is addressed as a prayer: "O myghty God, what shal he seye?" For the moment we are allowed to unite our detectivelike preoccupation with suspense and our role as lovers. We recover our sympathetically condescending protectiveness towards the lovers, as do the movers and shakers of Troy. For the purposes of the third book such poses are valid and, for the moment, without irony.

90

In the invocation to the third book the narrator calls upon Calliope, the muse of epic poetry, to provide him with a suitable voice. The book is dedicated to Venus. The question with which the narrator ended the second book, "what shal he seye?" speaking of Troilus, is applied to his own art, "How I mot telle anonright the gladnesse / Of Troilus, to Venus heryinge?" (III. 47-48). We are no longer addressed as student lovers or attendant clerks. This is poetry, the invocation seems to say, suddenly taking its subject, with what seems to be no irony, as a serious celebration of love. The images of the invocation— "In hevene and helle, in erthe and salte see," "Ye holden regne and hous in unitee"—reflect the apocalyptic blessedness with which a lover is wont to see the universe. We can drop our poses and become in this renewal an audience of celebration, following Venus' clerk in the service.

The opening scenes of the third book are serious in tone. Pandarus, to be sure, is involved in exaggerated poses, weeping loudly and poking his niece: "And Pandare wep as he to water wolde, / And poked evere his nece new and newe" (III. 115-116). But this a comic parody of Troilus' own grief and joy. Pandarus' speech to his niece is a bald commentary on Troilus' speech:

> Quod Pandarus, "Lo, here an hard requeste,
> And resonable, a lady for to werne!
> Now, nece myn, by natal Joves feste,
> Were I a god, ye sholden sterve as yerne,
> That heren wel this man wol nothing yerne
> But youre honour, and sen hym almost sterve,
> And ben so loth to suffren hym yow serve."
>
> (III. 148-154)

Pandarus assumes exaggerated poses, as if he were doing a dance that expressed the lovers' feelings:

> Fil Pandarus on knees, and up his eyen
> To heven threw, and held his hondes highe,
> "Immortal god," quod he . . .
>
> (III. 183-185)

91

He becomes a supplicant, mimicking the pose of the narrator; but as he does this, he directs the reader's attention to the lovers. Pandarus is beginning to become slightly irrelevant. He arranges the form of the lovers' meetings but has little to do with their content, and the interest of the reader in the third book is in the action, not, as in the second book, with the art of how it happens. Any identification we might have had with Pandarus' perspective on the action is qualified by his own quite dignified analysis of his position:

> ". . . for shame it is to seye:
> For the have I bigonne a gamen pleye,
> Which that I nevere do shal eft for other,
> Although he were a thousand fold my brother.

> "That is to seye, for the am I bicomen,
> Bitwixen game and ernest, swich a meene
> As maken wommen unto men to comen . . ."
> (III. 249-255)

Such will be Pandarus' unfortunate label in the popular mind. But the reader has also been between game and earnest and has also been participating in the fiction as a form of play. Pandarus' speech makes it clear that such participation can be foolery only up to an extent. After that, its moral repercussions can be serious. What he asks in the rest of his speech is that Troilus' behavior in some way protect Pandarus' moral investment, the self-respect he has gambled in this game. And indeed, in the rest of the book Troilus exceeds his friend's trust; he also redeems the reader's complicity in the plot. And for as long as he can, he does. It is not Troilus who fails us.

Everything in the third book asserts the centrality of the consummation scene, not the least of which is the scene's central location in the poem itself. The narrator's usually chatty refusals to describe things excessively suddenly takes on urgency. The obsession we were encouraged to have in the second book with time and place is replaced here by an almost musical movement towards a climax, attended by promptings that assert not so much the suspense as the almost ritual significance of this central episode: "Hadde out of doute a time to it founde," "A certayn houre, in which she comen sholde," "But at the laste, as every thing hath ende." The heavens, the weather, and history itself seem for the moment in a happy conspiracy.

It has been ably argued that the architectural setting of the love scene is borrowed from that of the fabliau. "Indeed," Charles Muscatine points out, "the bare mechanics of the bringing of Troilus to Criseyde could be constructed from just two fabliaux."[15] This is not what the reader is thinking of at this point, because the buildup of the love scene has tended to emphasize its profundity, in part by contrasting it with the antics of Pandarus and the misgivings of Troilus. Just as the courtly preconceptions of the audience were altered by the entrance of Pandarus in the first book, here the opposite happens. Our prurient and mundane reactions are transformed by the force of the poetry and the bliss of the lovers. It is not that the beauty of romance is undercut by the realism of the fabliau in this third book. Rather, the physics of the fabliau world are beatified by the metaphysics of the way in which the love is expressed.

The spatial arrangements with which the third book opens are those of the fabliaux. The world with which it ends is that of the *alba*, symbolized indeed by Troilus' song, but also by the actual parting speeches of the lovers. A number of critics, following Bedier, have pointed out the starkly functional mechanics of the fabliau setting.[16] There everything must have a practical object, for everything becomes part of the action. If a prop is needed, it is brought in at the necessary moment. The setting is created as it goes along, like a recipe—physical, domestic, practical. Jonathan Saville, in *The Medieval Erotic Alba*, has described the definite "world" that an *alba* projects. There the "interior" world, the chamber, is posited as a good. The world outside the lovers' room is "a world composed of everything that is not part of that love, a world that not only does not share the values of the world of love but is strongly opposed to them."[17] In a way, then, the reader's perception moves from the mechanical world view of the fabliau to the sacred and

93

fleeting isolation of the *alba*. Above it all, however, at least as expressed in the prevailing images of the third book, in the emotions of the lovers, and in the emotions of the narrator, is an almost romantic, apocalyptic notion of a universe ruled by love both inside and outside and above, which links the lovers implicitly to a divine ground of being. Perhaps, indeed, the world projected by the *alba* signals the fading of the "glimpse of heaven," which controls the center of the third book and returns us to the realization of the divisions that riddle this little earth.[18] By line 1490 we are in "this worldes tweyne." At any rate the reader's perception of the world shifts from that of a benevolent fabliau, to that of a divinely human comedy, to that of a nostalgic, bittersweet *alba*, looking back, rather than to the center of human existence.

Despite the warnings and our recognition of the poem's instability, there can be no underplaying the shock with which the reader faces the juxtaposition of Troilus' new refined manner at the end of the third book and the violence of the Trojan setbacks in the opening of the fourth book. We must reconsider our honestly romantic response to the third book and adapt, as protection, the "Jacobean" skepticism of the fourth book. There are many gods that fail in this poem, and in their wake they engender the awareness of corruption and failure that does indeed resemble that of Thersites.[19] Of course, we should have known better. The invocation to the fourth book lets us know what will happen. The action comes as no surprise. But the description of that action is as an exemplum of Fortune's behavior and has no greater force than one of the Monk's tragedies. At least it does not prepare the reader for the cruel experience of these books. The laughter of Fortune is addressed not only to the characters. There is an uncomfortable note of punishment at work in the fourth and fifth books, and it is directed against the reader as well as the characters.

If we have been lost in the timeless world of love in the third book, the battle scenes of the fourth book bring us back into history, and Calkas, again in a choral role, reminds us that history is eschatological:

94

"I have ek founde it be astronomye,
By sort, and by augurye ek, trewely,
And dar wel say, the tyme is faste by
That fire and flaumbe on al the town shal sprede,
And thus shal Troie torne to asshen dede."

(IV. 115-119)

The people whose "noyse . . . As breme as blase of strawe i-
set on fire" and the fire that will burn Troy are images that
remind us of the disaster that human reason and human passion
alone can only see as a conclusion to life. Troilus later swears
by the "fir and flaumbe funeral / In which my body brennen
shal to glede." It is as if the action that unfolds before us now
were lighted by that fire. When Troy was defending itself against
the Greeks, we saw little of it: a room here, a street scene there,
the chapel perhaps. But in the third book the city is idealized
as no city under siege could be:

In tyme of trewe, on haukyng wolde he ride,
Or elles honte boor, beer, or lyoun;
The smale bestes leet he gon biside.
And whan that he com ridyng into town,
Ful ofte his lady from hire wyndow down,
As fressh as faukoun comen out of muwe,
Ful redy was hym goodly to saluwe.

(III. 1779-1785)

The next book clearly announces that the truce is over. There
can be only brief respites from the usual course of history. This
book alerts us to the fact that human history can be no more
than the ebb and flow of disaster and destruction, of the best
intentions subverted by the facts of life. It alerts us too to the
problems of a storyteller who must give shape to a narrative
that proceeds from the chaos that history records.[20] The events
of Books IV and V seem sharply fragmented; time becomes
more difficult to ascertain. The locus shifts back and forth from
Troy to the Greek camp, suddenly illuminating an enemy world
that we were told about but had not seen and revealing the

95

dualism that we knew the world had all along, a self-defeating division, the double sorrow of history. The poet can give this narrative shape only by centering it on the story of lovers whose path parallels the path of history and by unfairly raising in the reader futile hopes about what merely human efforts can do for the course of history.

As the city is more direly threatened, as history intrudes on human love, Troy is revealed to us as more than a prop. The background in Book IV seems to take shape and move up behind the hero, disturbing the clear, isolated outline he once seemed to have. His actions are symbolic:

> He rist hym up, and every dore he shette
> And wyndow ek, and tho this sorwful man
> Upon his beddes syde adown hym sette . . .
> (IV. 232-234)

The outside world that had surrounded Troilus almost as an urban idyll now becomes a physical and mental threat.

Significantly, narrative interruptions are less frequent in the fourth book. This is partly no doubt why the course of the action is so painful. We are immersed in the linear stream of the fiction, without a guide to help us. We have art, said Nietzsche, to protect us from the truth. And the art of the narrator, which served constantly to remind us of the illusion of the story, did partly that. Now in the fourth book we are made to face the "reality" of what is happening. We are stripped of our protective distance and plunged into the story.

The trading of Criseyde incites a debate among various characters, the nature of which sheds light on some "illusions" held by characters within the narrative itself. Troilus' impulse is simply to save Criseyde. But his "resoun," by which self-counsel rather than rationality is meant, is to abide by the rules of courtly love and wait for her decision, which seems to rest on the fiction that she really has any choice. The almost scholastic logic that permeates the motivational monologues of courtly love characters returns to plague him again. He "gan deliberen, for the beste." Our rational response is to ask why he does not

simply stand up and claim Criseyde. But such reason is short-
circuited by Hector's noble cry, "Syres, she nys no prisonere."
Logic can only lead to the attitude of the mob, waspish and
cynical, which criticize's Hector's "fantasies." By all reasonable
counts, Antenor is the better choice.

The problem for the reader is expressed in a comment made
by the narrator, the meaning of which grows more and more
problematic as the poem moves towards its end. This comment,
although characteristically limited by the narrator to the citi-
zenry, is an unpleasant sort of pointing as far as the reader is
concerned:

> O Juvenal, lord! trewe is thy sentence,
> That litel wyten folk what is to yerne
> That they ne fynde in hire desire offence;
> For cloude of errour lat hem nat discerne
> What best is.   (IV. 197-201)

For the reader, the "cloude of errour" is the false perspectives
we have been compelled to take towards the story, changing
from pose to pose as the mood changes. "What best is," how-
ever, cannot be clear until the end of the narrative. And as
Criseyde begins to grow more and more like the image that
Henryson and Shakespeare would model their characters on,
the narrator's defense of her implants in our "reason" the no-
tion, like a demonic temptation, that she really is like that. The
baseness that we might share with the citizens of Troy is hinted
at.

The narrator has refused to describe certain things because,
as he tells us, we as lovers can imagine such and such far better
than he can. When the increasing tension of the plot builds in
the late second and early third books, he pushes on to the center
of the action, scorning irrelevant description. In the fourth book,
however, references to language, silence, and what speech can
communicate of the pathos of experience begin to sound in-
creasingly like bitter warnings rather than rhetorical ploys. To
Pandarus' ever-present strategic solutions to the problem at
hand, Troilus opposes a sharp and sympathetic skepticism:

"So hold thi pees; thow sleest me with thi speche!

Thow biddest me I shulde love another
Al fresshly newe, and lat Criseyde go!
It lith nat in my power, leeve brother;
And though I myght, I wolde nat do so.
But kanstow playen raket, to and fro,
Nettle in, dok out, now this, now that, Pandare?
Now foule falle hire for thi wo that care!"
                                                    (IV. 455-462)

Criseyde shows that she is inconsolable by means of a question
that mocks Pandarus' words of comfort. She addresses him as
if he were a classic bearer of bad news: " 'Allas!' quod she,
'what wordes may ye brynge?' " (IV. 857). But her speech in
fact asks for news of Troilus. For Troilus, however, rhetoric is
not only a form of obfuscation but a danger:

"Ye shal ek sen, youre fader shal yow glose
To ben a wif, and as he kan wel preche,
He shal som Grek so preyse and wel alose,
That ravysshen he shal yow with his speche . . ."
                                                    (IV. 1471-1474)

Finally, the narrator ends by admitting his inability to describe
Troilus' suffering:

For mannes hed ymagynen ne kan,
N'entendement considere, ne tonge telle
The cruele peynes of this sorwful man,
That passen every torment down in helle.
For whan he saugh that she ne myghte dwelle,
Which that his soule out of his herte rente,
Withouten more, out of the chaumbre he wente.
                                                    (IV. 1695-1701)

Chaucer implicates not only his art but our understanding.
Perhaps grief is not expressible but the reader's logical under-
standing of the story has in some way taken into account the

grief of these characters, however inexpressible that grief might be.

Qualifications of the efficacy of language and reason, and by extension the sorts of human happiness derived from them, occur most often in the fourth book. This is significant, almost symbolic, for it is here that the physical expression of despair dominates, even prevents the action. The book is filled with debate, both parliamentary and emotional, which seems to lead nowhere, or at least is of doubtful use against the force of time and history. The attacks on "logic" are not themselves merely rhetorical, for the use of reason and logic is the only defense the reader has left in the fourth book. The poet, and the chief characters, here qualify their use of language, as if to move from verbal art and narrative movement towards silence and stasis—perhaps to shore up defenses against the encroachment of time, but also to deny the movement of narrative, as if in protest against the preordained course of the plot.

For all the kindness and insinuating but self-mocking familiarity of the narrator, it is clear that Chaucer, as the prime mover behind all this, is marshaling a grimness worthy of Dante. C. S. Lewis long ago described part of this far better than I could:

> The species of suffering is one familiar to us all, as the sufferings of Lear and Oedipus are not. All men have waited with ever-decreasing hope, day after day, for some one or for something that does not come, and all would willingly forget the experience. Chaucer spares us no detail of the prolonged and sickening process to despair: every fluctuation of gnawing hope, every pitiful subterfuge of the flattering imagination, is held up to our eyes without mercy. The thing is so painful that perhaps no one without reluctance reads it twice. In our cowardice we are tempted to call it sentimental. We turn, for relief, to the titanic passions and heroic deaths of tragedy, because they are sublime and remote, and hence endurable. But this, we feel, goes almost beyond the bounds of art; this is treason.[21]

Lewis himself turns from this horror and reminds us again of the beauty of the first three books. With his usual unerring sensibility, Lewis was right about those books, at least in terms of effect. But that does not explain the last two books of the poem. Nor does it deny that the punishing experience that Chaucer inflicts on Lewis and us, and perhaps on himself, is planned and carried out with a truly furylike vengeance.

There is a new directness in the fifth book. In the fourth book the action was curiously static. But in the final book things begin to happen at once. There is not even an explicit invocation to this last book. The poet is suddenly an efficient man. Such efficiency, such directness and objectivity, is reflected in the famous series of portraits describing Diomede, Criseyde, and Troilus. The portraits in part distance the reader. Yet they seem also to reflect the tone of this book and its narrator. The narrator, who partakes a bit too heartily in the general mood of each of the books, here assumes a coldness and objectivity worthy of Diomede. He batters away at our defenses as ruthlessly as Diomede strips Criseyde of each of her hopes. His coldness, transformed by the Christian sentiment of the ending, becomes a form of divine omniscience.

The end of the poem is one of the few times Chaucer allows himself a truly apocalyptic perspective. The world of the poem seems to converge on Troilus, weighing him down. Coincidence, once a medium of joy for Troilus, is now a horrible nemesis, as he finds Criseyde's brooch. The "strokes" and "speres" that we always knew were there get ever closer, until "His lighte goost ful blisfully is went / Up"—and time is transmuted into space. Suddenly, everything is opened and illuminated. Troilus' laughter, which has any number of tones to it, also has a tone of exhilaration.

What follows is a literary technique that ought to be familiar to modern audiences. It is the sort of distancing technique that Brecht was fond of. Perhaps it is the necessary corollary of any ideological poetry, a recognition of what can or cannot be contained in fiction. The ending, rather than forcing upon us a Christian doctrine, impresses us with the extent to which we are incapable of a truly Christian attitude. We are made aware of the distance between our earthly strivings and the perfection displayed and generated by the figure of the last two stanzas. The process of the narrative, the act of reading or listening, involves the reader or audience in the exercise of that imperfection.

At the end, of course, Troilus looks down upon the scene of the story and perceives it "spatially." It is possible for the audience, and particularly for a reader, to share that vantage, at least after the story is over. Then we can see patterns and cross-references. While we are reading the poem, we can only understand its world through the partial perception of sequential development, for change and instability are at the heart of an imperfect world. In the empyrean, existence is changeless and eternal. Yet simply because that vantage is changeless, it cannot be explained in terms of a plot or a narrative; it is above such partial perspectives. A story happens in time. Its events unroll and must be put together, requiring a time-space continuum for their apprehension. We are forced to make sense of the action of a story, which can only be understood in terms of causal sequence.

As the audience finishes each phase of the narrative, it must question the validity of what has gone before. The events of the poem are in a certain fashion "self-consuming," as Stanley Fish has said of seventeenth-century prose.[22] But *Troilus and Criseyde* is also self-redeeming, for as we reach the end, it is possible to see the partial validity of each phase as just that, a partial validity. As Troilus rises above the mutable, created world, we are allowed a glimpse of what is above even his perspective. But just as Troilus must leave the world in order to see it as it really is, the reader must leave the story in order to perceive its truth, for some things cannot be said in a fictional world. As merely human love has limits, so does fiction. And with "wrecched worldes appetites" go also the "forme of olde clerkis speche / In poetrie, if ye hire bokes seche," which is a way of excusing but also condemning the narrative. What is remarkable here is that we are not only told that art has limits

101

but we are told what lies beyond those limits.[23] To transcend perception bound by this world requires an act of faith, a rejection in some way of the experience of the poem in order to understand it. However much one explains the ending, there is no rationalizing its shock and discontinuity for the reader. It is difficult to arrive at the conclusion that we need not feel sorry for Troilus, or for the world, or for that matter, for the poem. Our love of the story is a love of "kynde"; our understanding of it is a love "celestial," which is to say a love rooted in the intelligence. There are ways to synthesize them, of course, but an act of faith is required.

To the extent that narrative poetry is bound by perception in time, it is very much like the world itself, the image of the earthly world that Troilus looks down on at the end of the poem. Yet the world in time and the world beyond time are connected, and the link is clearly set out in the last stanza. The problem is that we, who live in time and understand by means of time, are not fit to understand the eternity of heaven. It would not be possible to gaze on the beauty of heaven directly; we must be led to that vision by means of time itself, for time will redeem us. The paradox of narrative in this sense resembles the paradox of Christian history. Discontinuity, foreshadowings, "spatial form," all the techniques of memory and interruption that are no doubt part of the arsenal of poets in any period, become in medieval narrative the way to truth. Just as the function of life on earth is to prepare us for the life beyond, for the vision of eternity, so is that of the narrative. The power of memory and the forms of understanding that we are allowed that transcend the tyranny of time are much like the techniques of this narrator. The poem gradually dazzles us with, and then divests us of, our own and the poet's best imaginings.

CHAPTER 4

Mannerism and Moralism in
Lydgate's *Siege of Thebes*

*T*he modern reader who turns to the *Siege of Thebes*, warily
enough, given the execration heaped upon its author's po-
etry and wit, is at first pleasantly surprised. There is something
bold and imaginative after all in writing another Canterbury
tale, this time following the pilgrims on their return from Can-
terbury and told by the author as if he were a character. Some
years ago, of course, the very attempt could be added to the
evidence for Lydgate's lack of originality, but the idea of imi-
tation has since crept back into modern fiction. We are at least
willing to listen. But such enthusiasm finds itself dissipated
almost immediately in confusions, which although harmless
enough, reveal both the sources and the limitations of Lydgate's
imagination.

Not the least extraordinary of these confusions is apparent
in the introductory passage itself, where the reality of narration
and the reality of fiction merge:

First the pylgrimes sothly euerichon,
At the Tabbard assembled on be on,
And fro suthwerk shortly forto seye,
To Canterbury ridyng on her weie,
Tellynge a tale as I reherce can,
Lich as the hoste assigned euery man
None so hardy his biddyng disobeye.
And this while that the pilgrymes leye

At Canterbury wel logged on and all,
I not in soth what I may it call,
Hap or fortune in Conclusioun,
That me byfil to entren into toun.
                              (Prol. 59-71)[1]

Perhaps the very fact of Lydgate's choosing to complete the *Canterbury Tales,* the oddly compelling sense of fulfillment that has the Canterbury pilgrims return home again (an idea that if Chaucer harbored it at all, he must have soon abandoned) causes us to overlook the shock of this transition. We have met the narrator and suddenly find him to be a character, but a character indistinguishable from the author. In a poet of more quickness and wit, we might take this to be a conscious ploy, an effort to play with our sense of illusion and our complicity in the fiction. Nothing could be further from Lydgate's imagination. He merely marches us into the frame here, without raising the question of whether literary people are meant to be real.

We find a number of such shifts of planes of reality in other poems, chiefly dream visions. Chaucer falls asleep reading Macrobius and wakes in a dream to meet Scipio himself. Dante comes across Ulysses and other fictional characters in the *Inferno.* It is not a question of the confusion of fable and history. In these other works we are at least prepared for the shift. In the *Siege of Thebes* it takes place without the slightest warning, without a word on the part of the narrator that we are on separate planes of reality. One of the chief literary effects of the *Canterbury Tales,* especially the frame, is that we are asked to accept the fictional reality of the pilgrims as people. They have literary archetypes, but they also possess a being as characters. There is no such invitation here. In the few lines preceding, Lydgate has praised Chaucer for the creation, or rather, the description of the pilgrims, for now they seem really to exist. But it is not a dream—it is a direct entry into the world of the pilgrims, without an indication of time or space to suggest their fictional quality. Indeed, even the distinction we make between Chaucer the poet and Chaucer the pilgrim seems unnecessary. For Lydgate the pilgrim and Lydgate the poet would in fact introduce the same kind of moralism into the work. The often inappropriate moral lessons to be drawn from certain episodes are not meant in the least to be ironic. The idea of challenging Chaucer on his own ground speaks directly to Lydgate's "anxiety of influence."[2] And it is not even that he has failed in his imitation. It is rather that he has acknowledged his debt by virtually becoming a character of Chaucer.

The basic element of Lydgate's imagination, and one that his audience apparently did not disapprove of, is his overwhelming literalism, his failure to acknowledge the interplay of different levels of reality or meaning. The voice that speaks to us speaks always in the same tone. The literalism is obvious even in the continuation of the device of the monk telling the tale, for we have specific details of time and place in the introduction to each part of the story, asking us to wait while we ride through a glen, carefully noting the time of day as the poet speaks on. It is a matter that Chaucer was far more careless about; the emphasis here seems to dictate a need for such reminders, a self-consciousness that belies the fiction of the speaking voice.

The means by which Lydgate gets himself invited among the pilgrims is worth a glance. There is something ambiguous about "tellynge a tale as I reherce can." Obviously it means that Lydgate knows the pilgrims; it is a compliment to Chaucer's ability to breathe life into his creations. But we have already moved into a different tense. The pilgrims are moving *now*. The cloudiness of all this is ignored in the next few lines, which emphasize the control of the host, as if this deftness could make up for the lack of clarity. The transitional line is extraordinary: "And this while that the pilgrymes laye." We are likely to ignore the torture of tense here as a stylistic mannerism, a way of filling the meter, until we realize a few lines later that we have left the time of the narrator's introduction and entered the time and the world of the pilgrims themselves. "While" here means a space of time, but the only indication that we have moved from the narrator's encomium to Chaucer to the

105

world of his fiction is the stop before this line, and that is not at all clear.

None of this is immediately disturbing. We are likely to dismiss it as a creaky mechanism. But it raises serious questions as to the authority of the poem. That is, Lydgate puts the *Siege* in this fictional frame, not to remove himself from the fiction and give himself more freedom and more protection against misinterpretation or offense as Chaucer did ("Blameth nat me"), but precisely for the opposite reason. As a rhetorical form the frame is meant to underline the seriousness of what the narrator is saying. It lends the story respectability. Instead of removing the stories from the aegis of doctrinal authority, the frame emphasizes the authority of the work. In Chaucer the frame displayed variations in reality and perspective. Here it memorializes a single point of view. For Chaucer the verisimilitude of the frame was a way of allowing play and irony in the world he creates. For Lydgate the frame eliminates the possibilities of irony and misinterpretation. By borrowing a form from Chaucer, he immediately establishes the seriousness of the endeavor, for to the fifteenth century Chaucer had become an authority as much as an entertainer.

The fictional possibilities of the frame are carefully constructed and then dropped. At the end of the poem, we do not return from the Canterbury journey. Instead Lydgate speaks to us in his own voice, putting the work within the scheme of Biblical history. Typical of Lydgate's style is this tendency to appropriate forms and images that suggest large vistas and complexities and then to retreat to certainties. To the modern reader part of the disappointment of Lydgate is this unfulfilled promise, which seems to be perversely abandoned. But another way of reading him is to see this leveling tendency as the very heart of his imagination, and that of his century.

THERE IS a certain danger in positing a revolution in literary sensibility at any time, as much as some critics would like to disassociate the work of Lydgate from the age of Chaucer. At the death of Chaucer, Lydgate would have been about thirty years old. To a certain degree his habits of mind and his literary style were already determined. All those influences, chiefly of reading and formal education, that we might take into account in considering Lydgate's poetic development had already been at work. The *Siege of Thebes*, dating from the 1420s and presumably mature Lydgate, is a reworking of an Old French prose romance that was based itself on a thirteenth-century *Roman de Thebes*.[3] Still, there is no doubt that Lydgate represents a change, partly with regard to his verse, which strikes us, coming from Chaucer and the *Gawain*-poet or from Gower, as irregular at best and hollow and repetitive at worst. It is as if one of Chaucer's characters had come to life and outlived him, and gone on and on, like Frankenstein's monster. Actually, the *Siege of Thebes* is not at all uninteresting or bad and might well deserve a modern edition. My aim here, however, is neither to bury nor to praise Lydgate, but to try to establish the importance and the meaning of his mannerism.

There is a certain uncomfortable strain in the criticism of Lydgate that seeks to ascribe his flatness, dullness, and (depending on the critic) either his incompetence or his excess of competence to his embarrassing enthusiasm for the taste and the politics of his patrons. I would argue that the reasons are far more general—located in the literary culture and society of the fifteenth century—and more specific—in the details of Lydgate's style. I would even suggest that there is a connection between the two. I do not want to argue that Lydgate is better than he is. Certainly he has strengths which for too long have been forgotten in a rain of witty dismissals; but attempts to resurrect him as an equal to, say, Gower are doomed to failure.[4] Without condescending to the taste of his age, a problem even in his defenders, it is possible to regard his most characteristic stylistic maneuvers as significant forms in themselves, which tell us a good deal about both the world of the poetry and the world that it speaks to. Lydgate's poetry does not, however, represent a treason of the clerks, an excessive willingness to tell people what they want to hear. True, there is less subversion in Lydgate than in Chaucer or Langland. And perhaps a measure

107

of subversion is necessary to what we regard as great art. It may well be that what we condemn as his tedium springs from the consistency of his intentions.

The art of Lydgate is as much a form of mannerism as the art that followed that of the Renaissance. It takes elements out of context and without appreciation for their original function and puts them in different places. It exaggerates certain elements. It projects a radically different relation of poet and audience. Of course, many mannerist expressions in the history of literature and art are more difficult to apprehend than their predecessors. Here it is Lydgate who is less obscure; his address to the audience is without irony and complication, though not without formal failings.

What I want to argue in this chapter on Lydgate, using the *Siege of Thebes* as my primary example, is that his often prolix narrative style, which cannot be honestly defended by any permanent scale of literary values, can be understood as part of a process of literary history that begins to include an audience broader than the court or the monastery. His style comes about from a union of—or rather a blurring of distinctions between—the perspectives of the court and the cloister. Part of his uniqueness is in his creation of a voice that could speak to prince and merchant on the same level.[5] Even given his extremely traditional origins, he achieved enormous popularity and helped to shape the taste of the fifteenth century. What I seek to describe, then, is this leveling tendency, which draws its power not from any new humanistic or democratic tendencies, but from the elaboration of elements to be found in courtly and monastic literature.[6]

Lydgate's style, in fact, springs from a number of discrete literary tendencies. It reveals a crisis in the adaptation of an oratorical literary style to a silent readership. It borrows from two fairly distinct conceptions of history, one that seeks to advise the prince in the management of earthly affairs, and one that regards all action in the earthly sphere as doomed to a cycle of decline; it combines, that is, an emphasis on predetermination with an emphasis on the moral quality of the participants in the story. At the same time that it offers advice to the prince, it suggests an ideal of social mores to an aspiring class of gentlefolk. It moves towards an analytical explanation of history at the same time that it confirms the timelessness of ideal qualities. Rather than move us between these contradictions or synthesize them into a new whole, however, Lydgate blithely merges them, and his style—garrulous, flowing, joining one event into the other, covering all emotions and incidents with repetitive and often tedious emphasis—is the agent of this merger. We are fixed in our positions towards the action of the poem. The image held before us is constantly guided by a voice as if from above.

Typical of Lydgate are certain habits of style, notable partly because they represent original contributions to his subject matter. One is a tendency to replace specific images with vague and less visual or tactile images. Today we are likely to regard such substitution with a grimace. The very heart of poetics for the past three-quarters of a century has been concreteness, and it is concreteness we look for in poets of the past. The romances of the late fourteenth and early fifteenth centuries, particularly those based on French romances, are filled with incredible detail, which is in effect a celebration and idealization of a certain style of life. It had the same effect that some advertising has today, particularly that for very expensive goods; it not only begs for new consumers but it congratulates those who already own the product. The long descriptions and catalogues of medieval romances were the culture's advertisements for itself. But this peculiar pleasure is missing from Lydgate's poem. It is replaced by less precise phrases and truncated description. Certainly conciseness is not Lydgate's aim; if it were, he would be even more monstrously bad than some of his critics claim. In fact, he takes longer to set out his description. Yet the image is usually vaguer. The medieval romance's characteristic celebration of the details of chivalric life is no longer of interest to Lydgate, either for reasons of obsolescence (there is gunfire in his battlefield) or because such details are of less interest than general values to a wider audience. I do not believe that medieval romance, except rarely, is allegorical. Nor do I think that Lydgate was trying to write an allegory. Rather he invests the actions of his narrative with a generalizing quality that resembles allegory. He has an exemplary imagination, though he usually tells us what the lesson is. But the figures themselves do not have the signification of allegorical figures; they merely partake of their generality. And it is in this broadness of application that Lydgate's appeal lies.

It is as if a romance were being preached at us rather than told to us. This is as it should be, one might think. For centuries the "Monk of Bury" had been Lydgate's heroic epithet. But in many ways the sermonlike air of the narration, its sense of being told to us from a position slightly above us in the moral world, is endemic not just to Lydgate but to a number of fifteenth-century poems. The relation of poet and audience becomes fixed in specifically didactic patterns. This does not exclude the poetry from a certain flexibility, but the manipulations available to such a rhetorical stance have a markedly declamatory tone.

The pulpit voice, of course, had always been part of the repertoire of medieval poets, and the sermon as an art form itself often rivaled romances in literary quality and liveliness. Indeed, the claim I made in chapter 1 is that the influence of popular sermon literature lent a richness and irony to earlier Middle English secular narrative. But now this tone dominates the rhetorical situation. The poet never leaves the pulpit, even when he pretends to, as Lydgate does here. Especially in England one could not always distinguish "pure" popular poetry or court poetry or moral poetry. Even when we can determine the specific impetus for the production of a medieval poem and know its immediate reception, we cannot always predict its impact on other audiences. Chaucer himself seems aware of that. And by the fifteenth century any work was destined for an audience of mixed composition, both on levels of class and levels of literacy.[7] Yet paradoxically, a new uniformity sets in, both in the style and rhetoric and in the tone of narration.

Even the tone and the variety of rhetorical devices the poet calls upon confirm this new relationship between poet and audience. A monumental scale, which some critics find lacking in fourteenth-century poetry, predominates. This monumentality does not provide, as Arnold might wish, high seriousness, however, for there is not enough relief, and when relief comes, it is trivial. Play and indirection are almost consciously removed. A poetry of irony becomes a poetry of emphasis. A poetry of implication becomes a poetry of explication.

ALTHOUGH FROM WHAT we can gather about Lydgate's sources, they were not as inflated as other romances in terms of long descriptions of battle and so forth, Lydgate clearly trims his descriptions of action at various points. The result is both a surprising concision, in which actions do seem subordinated to a larger purpose, and a distaste for the pleasure in splendor and violence and for the celebration of actions for their own sake. Whatever Lydgate's intention, however, it certainly is not narrative economy, for what marks these passages in most cases is expansion. The descriptions are abbreviated so that Lydgate can lecture at length on the moral import of the action. Even in brief descriptions of battles, he emphasizes not the actual danger and the violence being done, but the feelings aroused. The result is often his characteristic vagueness, but at other times an almost epic authority:

> And in despit who that was lief or loth,
> A sterne pas thorgh the halle he goth,
> Thorgh-out the courte and manly took his stede,
> And out of Thebes faste gan hym spede,
> Enhastyng hym til he was at large,
> And sped hym forth touard the londe of arge.
>   Thus leue I hym ride forth a while.
> Whilys that I retourne ageyn my style
> Vnto the kyng which in the halle stood
> Among his lordes furious and wood.
>
> (I. 2117-2126)

The measured brevity of the description suggests the majesty of the action. Lydgate's aim is probably not to suggest the narrative consequence of these councils, but to underline the essential makeup of Tydeus and Eteocles. It is not important that we are told twice that Tydeus leaves the hall, at least not for the story, for he will soon be waylaid. What is important is the contrast between "sterne" and "manly," "furious" and "wood." The abbreviation emphasizes Lydgate's interest in the primacy of character and in the abstract principles of behavior that for him make up character, not in economy of expression. Indeed, everywhere throughout Lydgate's work there is a tendency for instruction to replace the social concerns of romance. Interest is not in the celebration of class, but in the judgment of individual character.

Significant too in this passage and in the lines immediately surrounding it is the emphasis not on the actions of Tydeus and Eteocles, but on the words these characters use and the words used to describe them. The transitional device ("I retourne ageyn my style") is entirely conventional and almost seems stilted until we concentrate on the redemptive value of abstract words in the entire debate. The question is whether Eteocles will alternate rule with his brother as he has agreed, and the debate is expressed in terms of honor, agreement, and values. Yet Eteocles' intemperate rage far exceeds any subtlety in his character, and Tydeus seems like an exemplary figure. Usually the emphasis is on the actions of exemplary characters; here, more importance is attached to the words that describe the actions. It is almost as if the timeless and stable values that abstract words project are good, or at least safe from the ravages of change, whereas action itself can only lead to tragedy. Indeed, throughout the poem stasis and passivity and agreement are made to seem good, whereas violent actions, no matter how necessary, are bad. The aim of Lydgate's narrative style, with its repetition and its tendency towards vagueness and abstraction, is not to imitate action in the physical world, but to emphasize the words that are used to describe each action. His style is thus rhetorical in the most didactic sense, not mimetic or even narrative. The action of the narrative, sometimes against its most obvious import, is made subsidiary to the words and the moral abstractions. Everywhere in the poem events are made

112

to fit an emblematic pattern instead of generating their own
meaning.

A few lines later, of course, Tydeus fights his way out of an
ambush. We are told that in escaping he killed fifty knights,
leaving one who returned to tell Eteocles of the failure of his
treachery. Yet in the stanza after this we are told the same thing
again:

> By which ensample ye opynly may se
> Ageynes trouthe falshed hath no myght.
> Fy on querilis nat grounded vpon right,
> with-oute which may be no victorye.
> Therefor ech man haue this in memorye,
> That gret pouer shortly to conclude,
> Plente of good nor moche multitude,
> Scleight or engyne fors or felonye,
> Arn to feble to holden Chanpartye
> Ageynes trouthe who that list take hede.
> For at the ende falshede may not spede
> Tendure longe ye shul fynde it thus.
> Record I take of worthy Tydeus,
> which with his hand thorgh trouthes excellence,
> Fyfty knyghtes slogh in hys dyffence.
>   (I. 2236-2250)

Lydgate is as fond of repeating incidents as he is of repeating
words. Repetition of incidents is common enough in romances;
it serves to recapitulate the plot, to catch up late members of
the audience in oral presentation, to emphasize the importance
of the action in some cases; sometimes if the hero tells what
he has done, it is a way of confirming his identity. But here
the same information is given to us a second time by the nar-
rator. The reason seems clear: it provides Lydgate with a chance
to ascribe a moral significance to the earlier action. Truth always
will out. The impulse towards moralization in such a case bears
a trace of anxiety. Lydgate retells the story of Tydeus' escape
at the end of the stanza as if he were embarrassed at the break
in the narration. But he seems to be rational enough to feel a

113

bit upset about what is after all a typical romance action. It is nothing to kill fifty knights single-handedly in any number of romances. But for Lydgate, the action requires explanation—moral, not physical or supernatural explanation. By raising the admirable Tydeus to a moral abstraction, Lydgate obscures the equivocal morality of the action itself. We see exhibited here the same split that besets Lydgate's other repetitions and emphases. We have one version of the story that emphasizes physical action and heroism that will ultimately result in tragedy, and we have another that emphasizes moral qualities that we can apply to our own lives. It is style of narrative with a double vision, but the boundary between those visions is obscured.

Despite the havoc such a stylistic tendency wreaks with form, it allows Lydgate a certain monumental scope that has some potential for full development, though he rarely takes advantage of it. For one thing, such a style puts public action and morality and private action and morality on the same level. The equivalence between such spheres may well be at the heart of the very myth of Oedipus and Thebes that this narrative retells. Lydgate's style, by retaining its abstract and ideal quality and making its point through repetition and emphasis rather than precise image, may test the patience of the modern reader, but it also achieves a curious moral balance: it is able to describe and to some extent celebrate action in the earthly world, while at the same time displaying that world's ultimate futility. Even the most moralistic reader, after all, might find himself engaged by the stirring description of a battle or a pageant that adorns so many medieval narratives. There is always the danger of such an enticing description creating its own ethical values. But Lydgate's kind of description never lets us forget the ideals behind the action.

Such a style, however crudely, includes its own analysis within its description of events. Nothing is left without a demarcation of its ethical and ideal value. Many medieval poems do in fact seem to include their own commentary. But in the *Siege of Thebes* the commentary almost takes over as the essential part of the poem. For all its limitations, such a habit of mind has a number of affective repercussions. It does, as I have just said, simultaneously celebrate and denigrate human action in the earthly world. But it also moves towards a sense of earthly action interpreted by a real scale of values and expectations. It allows a form of political interpretation. Of course, Lydgate's interpretation is profoundly monastic and medieval, but the framework for a kind of interpretation that would eventually appeal to a new readership is here.

Even the potentially absurd motivations of romance are as-similated into an ethical framework:

> And in this whil, of Rancour rekkeles,
> Out of Thebes rood Ethiocles,
> And with him ek, the worthy kyng Tremour,
> Of his hond a noble werreour,
> That made Grekes to forsak her place,
> And to her tentys gan hem to enchace.
> And myd the feld as thei to-gyder mette
> On hors-bak with speres sharpe whette
> Of verray hate and of envious pryde,
> Ful many on was ded on outher syde.
> The whiche thyng whan Tideus espieth,
> wood as lyoun to horsbak he hieth.
>
> (III. 3893-3904)

Again an act of violence is a turning point in the action, and again we find a noteworthy restraint on the part of the poet. When we read a few lines later, "many on lay slayen at the gate / Gapyng vprightys with her woundys wyde," it is to em-phasize the rage of Tydeus. Unlike some poems, which pretend to condemn war while secretly gloating over it, Lydgate recounts his incidents without glorification. It is in the nature of his style, which has the drawback of being imprecise, to express the limitations of this kind of behavior. It does so with a tone of weariness and resignation. It allows, that is, Lydgate to be both royal advisor and monastic fabulist at once. Here too the nobility of the characters is emphasized along with their vain course of action. Instead of indulging in the luxury of the details

115

of battle scenes, no small temptation for a poet of such prolixity, Lydgate emphasizes words, and words that express ideal behavior, so that the description might be of allegorical battles: "Rancour rekkeles," "worthy," "noble," "verray hate," "envious pryde," "wood as lyoun"; fully a third of the stanza consists of abstract words that denote abstract qualities. Such description serves to acknowledge and celebrate the limits of such qualities, but it does so by a dry tone and vagueness rather than irony or precision. The language itself explains the actions, which are not allowed to speak for themselves. Indeed, on this level, the thoroughly absurd catalyst that initiates the battle is irrelevant: the fighting starts because the pet tiger of the Thebans is allowed to roam loose among the Greeks, who panic and slay it. By a reasonable standard of causation the incident is absurd, almost comic. But the real motivation, as Lydgate sees it, is the abstract qualities of characters and events. The idealism implicit in all medieval romances is removed from its class basis, and the ethical abstractions that remain are used to interpret the world.

That Lydgate's own values are medieval and traditional and that he regards the ultimate result of earthly action as hopeless is without question. But his tendency to moralize sometimes gives one a different impression. For one thing, as we have seen, it provides a vocabulary to weigh the relation between personal, political, and historical forces. Lydgate himself often sees this relation as foolish and beside the point, and that is part of his problem. The bizarre gap between his commentary and the events he is describing speaks to a crisis in values. Part of his urge to pile on explanations derives from a nagging sense that these explanations do not explain anything at all. Such ambiguous explanations encourage the reader to provide discrete interpretations for each event, and in so doing reveal a crisis that will only be resolved much later with the development of modern historical explanation. In the consistently leveling quality of Lydgate's style and in the vagary of his explanations we begin to see evidence of a larger crisis: the contradiction of a culture that has already begun to think in ways that will form the germ of modern political and scientific thought but that clings for justification to traditional, though highly exaggerated, medieval forms.[8] In no sense is Lydgate's imagination akin to that of the secular humanists of the Renaissance or to modern historiographers, but he does make evident a crisis from which these developments grow.

TO SAY THAT Lydgate's poetry contains its own commentary is not a metaphoric way of begging off the possibility of criticism. Rather, it is to say that the tone of Lydgate's work demands a response that the modern reader usually reserves for a literature of statement and fact, not one of fiction. It is a commonplace of literary histories that medieval genres made no such squeamish distinctions. Indeed, contemporary writing in the last few years has crossed the boundaries of fiction and nonfiction, and we are less likely to demand such purism. There is good evidence in the poem to suggest that Lydgate regarded the matter of Thebes as history as well as fiction, or rather that one could draw equally upon history and fiction to support a moral position. The events of the story are shaped to support the moral generalizations imposed by his commentary. The poetics of the poem finds its origins in forensic and deliberation. Even within a few hundred lines, we learn the theme of envy and rule that will run like a commercial advertisement through the work. The characters and events thus draw their logic from the imposed moral order rather than from their internal consistency or our identification with them, or even from the irony of plot, something the Theban legend has in more than abundance. Thus the work, as a reading experience, more resembles nonfiction prose than poetic fiction. We are made to move from significance to an appreciation of the natural form, instead of apprehending significance through form. Something of the sort could be said of much medieval literature to the degree that it is all didactic. But rarely, save in moral tracts themselves, does one find such elaborate moralization of incident on such a scale. Furthermore, in the best medieval fictions one finds characters moving independently of an imposed moral order, so much so that in

117

Chaucer, for instance, we are made to experience the independent life of the characters as part of our apprehension of the poem's meaning. In Lydgate whatever illumination the story reveals is a product of the overwhelming marshaling of moral discourse beyond the plot itself.

We have come a long way in the understanding of medieval rhetoric since the days when it was dismissed as an unnecessary decoration, more an obfuscation than a part of the meaning. Yet particularly in the criticism of Lydgate one finds the old prejudices reinforced. His elaborations and sonorous empty lines are now and again pointed out. But a few recent critics have tried to counter these attacks: Renoir and Schirmer have tried to point out the appropriateness of some of Lydgate's rhetorical flights. Pearsall has suggested a rather different view, emphasizing the importance of rhetorical elaboration in the discovery of English as a literary language and the epistemological qualities of that rhetoric. In Lydgate's tendency to respond automatically to any situation with topics of all sorts, one finds life being regulated by ordered, immutable categories.

To the degree that such a description of Lydgate is accurate, it implies a radically different use of rhetoric than we saw in the writers of the fourteenth century, though in the long view it seems to be the fourteenth-century poets who are the exceptions to the rule. In Chaucer and the *Gawain*-poet the order implied by the processes of rhetoric was questioned, sometimes by the consequences of the action, sometimes by intricacies within the rhetoric itself. Always the purpose of that style was an unsettling questioning of the gap between how things seem and what they are. In Lydgate rhetoric is used to emphasize a direct connection, not an ironic distance, between appearance and reality. It constantly emphasizes, clarifies, and interprets. Since it provides interpretation directly, we are not asked to gather the implications ourselves. It is not that Lydgate is completely incapable of creating a form that generates its own meaning. A case could be made that the slow, destructive course of history is encompassed in the leisurely pace and monumental length of the Troy book. But in the *Siege of Thebes* the conception of poetry is clearer. The form itself is not seen to have a significant epistemological function; always categories and meanings must be imposed from above. Everywhere in the poetry of Lydgate—in the rhetoric, in the moral elaborations, even in the statements of the characters themselves—one finds an obsession with justification, as if an anxiety about legitimacy and order were spread to anxiety about language and fiction.

That Lydgate's repetition and vagueness dull our mind is testament to a different conception of poetry as well as to a failure of skill on the part of the poet. It also, however, presumes an appetite for such literature, an appetite whose taste is literally created by poetry such as Lydgate's. He regards himself, not wrongly, as a teacher, but what he teaches is less morality than a love for moralization. Even the expansiveness of his works suggests this. The more morality, the less specific, the better. The usual advice to the prince is couched in terms that might provide food for thought and manners and guidance for those such as the landed gentleman. The possession of books might be more important than their form. Having a large book full of morality may reflect well on one's morals. Like much of Lydgate's work, the *Siege of Thebes* bears a curious middle ground between artifact and performance.

At the same time, the flaccid rhetoric that derives from the traditions of medieval style and system threatens that very system and style, for that world view depends on distinction, hierarchy, and equivalence. Lydgate preaches fidelity to that system, but his lack of discrimination jumbles the elements. If anything marks Lydgate's style, it is the blurring of distinctions. In syntax, images, and elaborations of all sorts it is often difficult to tell where one element begins and the other leaves off. Something of this happens in, say, Langland, but there, I think, the point is to make us question the validity of logical inquiry unaccompanied by a constant consciousness of the unity and vision necessary to faith. In Lydgate there is a different source and a different point. His elaboration of medieval system moves in two equally decadent directions, collapsing on the one hand of its own weight, floating away on the other in consequence

119

of its own abstraction. Making us question our understanding or in any sense invalidating the structures he has created is the farthest thing from Lydgate's mind. The aim of his style is to remind, instruct, and emphasize, to keep moral categories continually within our vision. It is as if a building had grown weaker and weaker and had to be supported by more and more buttresses, to the point where the buttresses interfere with the uses of the building.

This is not merely to say that Lydgate lacked irony. The point is that the force of Lydgate's style seems aimed at *preventing* a certain kind of irony, as if any gap between intention and comprehension would be a literary and moral failure. Everywhere there is evidenced an anxiety to insure that the stance of the poet and the stance of the audience are the same. Indeed, Lydgate's rambling sentences often seem to be literally attempts to shepherd our responses. In earlier chapters I argued that medieval fiction, especially when it dwells on secular plots, is implicitly ironic. It partakes, that is, of a form of cosmic irony in attempting to give form to a series of phenomena that are by definition inexplicable from an earthly perspective. The poet attempts to orient events in a linear, logical sequence, which is in itself a pale imitation of the instantaneous apprehension of his Creator. The poet could in fact play upon this difference, as Dante and Chaucer did. One could merely decry it, or ignore it, as a number of lesser poets did. Yet the effect of Lydgate's style is rather paradoxical. On the one hand, his moral interruptions serve to break up the causal connection between events; we are asked to see them as discrete moral problems. Yet the flowing quality of his style serves to bring them in line with each other, as if all levels of existence were equally valid in terms of their exemplary import. Furthermore, his pedantic streak, his tendency to fill in information and even dates and times, as if to plead the veracity of his story—or perhaps to excuse a classical, pagan tale as his matter—has the effect of inducing a historical consciousness instead of contempt for the hapless cycle of battles and treacheries. Clearly, Lydgate's intention, as Ayers pointed out, was to modernize the classical figures of the plot in order to transfer their moral meaning to his audience.[9] That is, the characters are generalized to insure their wide application. To a smaller degree, the opposite effect also is at work: the moralization becomes a form of perception and interpretation that makes the characters' actions understandable and thus moves towards a kind of historical analysis. In any case, to say that Lydgate's imagination is prosaic is not entirely a slur. It is meant to suggest that he regards his fictions as evidence rather than as entertainment.

The events that Lydgate narrates do not acquire their significance from a satisfying aesthetic form or from their inner continuity. Instead, his incidents are presented as part of a large marshaling of examples, which derive their importance from their reference to an explicit moral structure. Indeed, Lydgate seems to connect incidents by appealing to the reader's moral understanding. The means by which this is accomplished is irony, not emphasis, repetition, not understatement. Much late medieval narrative derives its sense of form from romance; Lydgate seems to draw upon such genres as encyclopedias or universal history for his sense of form. Such a form attempts to include within itself all the knowledge of Christendom, both to display the glory of its own tradition and to protect that tradition against attack and misuse. The result, in Lydgate, is a formidable strength and massiveness. Yet behind that massiveness is a certain defensive anxiety, and in that anxiety Lydgate seems to forego the great advantages of the system he seeks to defend, such as its order and structure. If the work achieves any real coherence, it does so only by the leveling style of the poet—at the cost, that is, of the liveliness and inventiveness of voice, which is one of the great delights of Middle English poetry—and by the embryonic sense of history that is implicit in the massiveness and flow of the poem itself—at the cost, that is, of the poem's message about the futile contradictions of human history. There is a good deal to the conviction that Lydgate's kind of poetry is a reaction, a retreat to medieval certainties, rather than a transition to humanism. But Lydgate's poetry is as little served by the notion of reaction as it is by

121

the notion of a transition to humanism. All the great themes of medieval poetry are here, but they seem not to hold together, except by reference to an order in the reader's moral response, which itself seems here to require inordinate support. Rather, the lack of convincing structure in Lydgate is a symptom of a system in collapse, but a collapse that his style seeks desperately to forestall.

The Limits of Vision in Henryson's
Testament of Cresseid

*b*enryson's remarkable poem, the *Testament of Cresseid*, has traditionally been understood as a continuation of and homage to Chaucer's *Troilus*. Recent scholarship has also tried to place it in the context of fifteenth-century ideas and the Scots literary climate.[1] What I propose to argue here is slightly different. It is that the very strengths of Henryson's art depend at least partly on the characteristic failures of fifteenth-century poetry in general. What the poem offers is less a narrative or a clear moral message than a corrective reading experience, an antidote to a century of excess or defect.

Indeed, part of the debate about the poem's meaning or moral position derives from a paradox at the heart of its form. On the one hand, the work manifests a fixity, a conciseness, and a structure that implies an equally fixed and reliable moral order.[2] At the same time, the poetry utilizes to the fullest a range of references, rhetorical devices, and a flowing relativism and subordination that suggests an almost humanistic flexibility.

Yet the uses of both tendencies, the fluid style and the ordered structure, are limited in the *Testament* not only by their struggle with each other but by literary convention itself, that is, by the historical development of form and style in the fifteenth century, both in England and France, a context certainly as important as the native Scots literary situation. Beneath the imposing edifice of Henryson's work we are able to identify a bewildering array of different literary forms, to the extent that it seems as if the work verges on becoming a pastiche of any number of possible genres: complaint, tragedy, romance, testament, and so forth. Literary forms are ways of explaining experience. Indeed, they offer a kind of contract between author and reader: we agree to see what this form allows us to see; we agree not to bring in inadmissible evidence. In return, we expect a certain pattern of experience. Most significant works play with these expectations. But the shifting permutations in Henryson's *Testament* amount to a critique of that contract. He is saying that none of these conventions sufficiently communicates the reality of experience. We do learn something of the limitations of literary forms to communicate experience from reading Chaucer's *Troilus*; no doubt Henryson did too. Chaucer's style, however, depended on our flow of sympathy and empathy. To a much greater degree Henryson imposes checks on our emotional response.

One of the characteristic vices of fifteenth-century literature is the wholesale replication of forms, themes, symbols, and images, with less than full appreciation of their proper uses and sense.[3] What Henryson has done is merge a series of forms into an imposing imitation of order. It holds together not by system and structure, but by a kind of yoking. In its search for an appropriate form such a façade creates a false impression of strength. The *Testament* does not offer a synthesis of literary traditions and themes so much as it exploits their exhaustion. Themes one could find endlessly duplicated in fifteenth-century poetry in at least three languages are incorporated here, executed beautifully; they offer their insight into experience and then pass away. They neither strengthen nor deny the theme that has just been offered to us, for to admit association would be to reveal their incompatibility. The structure of the poem announces a rigid moral order because it can afford no other.

Even the style of the *Testament* seems to prescribe its own limits. Henryson exhibits considerable mastery over his rhetoric and pace. Indeed, control is the key to the work.[4] Henryson has perfect control over movement within a stanza, but each stanza seems self-contained. The sonorous style pulls us into the poem at various points but precludes questions at other points, precisely when human reactions are open to question. To understand Henryson's method we must be aware of the extended pathos of fifteenth-century poetry, in which prolixity is both a mode of emphasis and a way of escaping serious questions by drowning them in excess. Henryson seems to recognize the vacuity of a kind of poetry that would devalue experience by endlessly duplicating the forms that had been invented to express it. His solution is to short-circuit our response, allowing us neither the escape of dulling repetition nor the luxury of pathos.

There is a profound way in which the narratives we have examined from the fourteenth century are radically experiential. Their effect on us comes in good part from our identification with the experiences and with the nuances of emotion of the characters. This is not merely a way of saying that they are better or more modern than fifteenth-century works. It allowed Chaucer, say, to portray his characters for their humanity as well as for the sake of some larger constellation of values. Henryson's art consists in a great measure of the creation of an image for our contemplation. The crucial part of the work is the heroine's address to us, which, unlike similar statements of remorse by Chaucer's Criseyde, does not acquire its resonance from our knowledge of her emotions and experience.[5]

Everywhere in the *Testament* there is a tendency to limit the reader's response. Of course, no poem can succeed without being to some extent evocative; the reader must be allowed to respond to suggestions made by the poem. The measure, after all, of a writer who trusts his own art is how much he trusts his reader. And there are more than enough unanswered questions in the *Testament*. But where Chaucer could predict and suggest various responses, the rhetoric of the *Testament* returns us to the main point of the story. It is finally terrible in its concentration. The frequent interruptions of the narrator, and his refusals to elaborate, do not actually inhibit our responses, but they make it clear that we follow such leads without the authority of the poem itself. For an audience who would be likely to extend the emotional impact of the poem's plot into the realm of the sentimental and who might well be fascinated at the horror of its events, without calling into question the logic of its justice, the very concentration of the poem is a radical form of meaning.

The poem itself projects a limited world, despite its apparent sweep from the heavens to the encircling camp to the borderland of the lepers, for in all these places, our only sense of space is enclosed rooms, which seem virtually to imprison us. We meet the narrator in his cold, dark study. Cresseid herself undergoes most of her experience in her room. Calchas is called from the dining chamber. Cresseid's place among the lepers is a "dark room and alone." Even the parliament of the Gods takes place in what seems to be a chamber of some sort, though it is never localized. The transitions between these scenes are abrupt, as if to suggest the continuity of these worlds. The major scene, which occurs out-of-doors, with Troilus riding past the lepers, takes place within the shadows of the walls of the city. The limits of space, like the limits of language and the compressed sense of time, increase our feeling of being hemmed in, of possibilities and meanings closed off, of the hopelessness of escape.

Our response to such a world is not to enter it, but to look into it, as into a *camera obscura*. We might look up at it, down at it, or directly across at it, as the levels of style demand, but rarely is our perspective itself radically shifted. We are fixed in our relation to the action. The art of the poem does not consist, as did that of the previous century, in questioning the validity of our perception. It in fact limits its own world to the scope of our realm of vision. Any dissatisfaction we feel with that limitation is problematic, but the poem leaves us with the problem rather than resolving or even addressing it.

If, as I have argued, the art of the late fourteenth-century masters consisted in questioning values that earlier poets had left alone, that of the fifteenth-century poets is different. The introduction of a given theme leads to a replication, which breeds satiety and exhaustion. The dose must be increased each time. But Henryson reasserts the need for proportion and limits.

126

Everywhere in his style there is a tendency to limit the response of the audience, and at the same time to limit the possibilities of his own kind of poetry.

BECAUSE THE compression of the *Testament* is so notable, the transitional scenes, the very seams of the work, repay careful attention:

> The day passit and Phebus went to rest,
> The cloudis blak ouerheled all the sky.
> God wait gif Cresseid was ane sorrowfull gest,
> Seing that vncouth fair and harbery!
> But meit or drink scho dressit hir to ly
> In ane dark corner of the hous allone,
> And on this wyse, weiping, scho maid hir mone.
>
> $$(400\text{-}406)^6$$

The scene is the leper colony, to which Cresseid has just been transported, and what follows is her famous complaint. The lines that take us there are worth reading carefully, because they reflect the peculiar modulations of the entire work. Such transitional formulas as this are entirely conventional; we could draw from fifteenth-century narratives any number of examples of the hero or heroine about to turn in for the night under the aspect of some astrological sign. But the conditions here are different, for the significant action has already taken place. What follows is Cresseid's resignation to her fate. Thus the conventional rhetoric of the passage acquires an unusual irony. Furthermore, Phebus' going to rest ushers in not a peaceful night, but a horrid recognition and a welcome cloak of darkness. The very neutrality with which the action of the god is described is noteworthy. Phebus' journey is not meant merely to elevate through rhetoric the description of time or to impress upon us the importance of the moment alone, although it does that too as a fitting introduction to Cresseid's aria. We have met Phebus already, as a character and as a mechanical device, and the effect of the convention is now no longer abstract.

127

Against the grandiloquence of these lines, we must contrast the horror of Cresseid's situation; against their casualness, the result of their influence. The next two lines carry on that casualness with a note of almost unpleasant irony. Cresseid is a "sorrowfull gest," partly because of the poor conditions of her rooms mentioned in the next line, but surely her existential situation is more significant than the lowering of her estate. It is as if there were an equivalence suggested between the setting and Cresseid's moral state. Such an equivalence is made more explicit in the splendid resonance of the next line: "In ane dark corner of the hous allone." The dark corner is a proscribed place a long way from the great sweep of the sun described in the first line. As we move towards the human world, our vision becomes not just blurred by darkness but limited in space. The self-contained nature of the stanza is emphasized, not broken, by the fact that the narrator must devote the last line to introducing Cresseid's speech. Such self-conscious transitions are necessary to break the boundaries of the stanza, the form of which is a sustained, self-enclosed address to the audience. It is as if the narrator were showing us the action as an emblem or a masque. The style of the stanza is a grand movement from the high rhetoric of the first few lines to the humility of the simple house, the poor food, the dark corner, the tears, and the isolation. The language moves us from the consideration of the world to the contemplation of our place in it.

One of the ironies of Henryson's *Testament* is that control and consciousness of language, both for the poet and for his characters, seem to increase as the horror of what is happening begins to dawn on the reader. The conciseness that Spearing has noted in Henryson is evident, but the tone is more difficult to describe. It is not at all clear whether his concentration and straightforwardness are matters of stiff-lipped sympathy with his heroine or rhetorical understatement or are curious reflections of the callousness of his gods. The passage below is both summary and transition. Sentence has been passed upon Cresseid, and Saturn is to pass this on to her, judgment and execution at once:

> Than thus proceidit Saturne and the Mone
> Quhen thay the mater rypelie had degest:
> For the dispyte to Cupide scho had done
> And to Venus, oppin and manifest,
> In all hir lyfe with pane to be opprest,
> And torment sair with seiknes incurabill,
> And to all louers be abhominabill.
>
> This duleful sentence Saturne tuik on hand,
> And passit doun quhair cairfull Cresseid lay,
> And on hir heid he laid ane frostie wand;
> Than lawfullie on this wyse can he say:
> 'Thy greit fairnes and all thy bewtie gay,
> Thy wantoun blude, and eik thy golden hair
> Heir I exclude fra the for euermair.'
>
> $$(301\text{-}315)$$

Again we find that which is most typical of the poet's vision included in those passages in which the mortal and the immortal cross paths. Implicit in the irony of the above passage is the degree to which the various characters are subject to the laws of time and change. The matters of justice and power that are at the heart of the critical debate surrounding the work are here implicit too. Cresseid does not on the one hand seem to deserve such treatment, but she is not blameless. We are asked to observe an act of pagan justice through our perspective of Christian mercy.[7] Even within the structure of the narrative the reversal is expressed, for this passage gives us the turning point of the action: the characters of the gods appear as within a dream, created as if by Cresseid herself. But the power is theirs, and the dream ends by having the creatures of her vision turn on her. The manner in which Henryson accomplishes this serves to summarize the strategy of the poem.

There is an offhand and leisurely quality to the first two lines of this passage—"than thus . . . Quhen thay . . . had degest,"—that suggests an almost impartial quality in the justice that is being dispensed, as if the fury of the gods' revenge had been somehow purified by the legal apparatus that they have

129

just gone through, which is after all a kangaroo court. It is almost as if the gods needed such justification, as indeed from a Christian perspective they do. But the coldly executive quality of this transitional phrase implies a kind of inhumanity that only humans can aspire to. The diction—"proceidet," "mater," "oppin and manifest"—is not only logical but administrative and legalistic, the kind of language humans use when they want to disguise their own passions or when they have no idea what the results will be. The disturbing thing about Henryson's gods is not the ways in which they are godlike, but the ways in which, like the gods of Ovid and of Euripides, they exhibit a certain human pettiness. Power is more naked here than in the similar debate in *The Knight's Tale*.

Even as the sentence is being formulated in the second half of the stanza, the limited nature of Cresseid's crime is emphasized ("dispyte"); but since the rhetoric is in that administrative style, it leaves less room for qualification than we would like. The narrator's silence is more troubling than his interruptions. There is a large, resonant quality to the last two lines of the first stanza quoted above, which echo with long Latinate words— "incurabill," "abhominabill"—giving a grandiosity to this terrible judgment and emphasizing its finality and the authority of its source. The more human words in the stanza—"torment sair," "pane," "lovers"—suggest the suffering rather than the agent, yet they seem incommensurate with what is happening, partly because the gods are immune, partly because the suffering is so grotesque, and partly because the punishment is so creatural. The humanized words, after all, are human here because they are the words used to describe the loss of love in courtly love poetry. And that, ironically, is what Cresseid has caused, not what she has suffered.

In the stanza that precedes the passage quoted above Saturn's movements are described in the same leisurely manner that is used in the first two lines of the above quoted stanzas. Here there is a certain majesty to his movement. He is indeed the judge, and not just the deliberator. In some ways he seems to manifest more of the attributes of Jupiter than Jupiter himself;

there is a kind of statuesque magnificence to his figure, with the judgment in one hand and the wand in the other. The "frostie wand," however, recalls his portrait in its gruesome detail and reminds us too of the grotesque actions that are to follow. It is fitting that the god who is the ugliest and the oldest should pass judgment, significant too that the judgment should be one that age will bring to all men and women in any case, and one that recalls both the cold that permeates the prologue and the age of the narrator. There is something magical about the action: it resembles oddly an incident from romance, an enchantment.

Saturn speaks "lawfully," but there is a cold passion behind his words. His speech in the stanzas quoted above shows Henryson's ability to take the commonplaces of fifteenth-century poetry, which in another context would be moribund and make them come alive. The themes of *ubi sunt* and *memento mori* usually reverse the blandishments of courtly love poetry—we see the flowers as they pass. But here the Latinate "exclude" and the judgmental "wanton" as well as the second-person address lend an immediacy and a compression that courtly love poems rarely have. The poetry and paradox of line 314 are even more ironic in Saturn's voice. Perhaps all the "lovers" in the audience will someday be subjected to the terrors of the flesh that will render them "abhominabill," but our pity for Cresseid derives from the fact that her situation depends on her complicity, not on her existence.

There is a further poignancy in that Cresseid's punishment is not only physical and moral but social. She has to leave even the little comfort she has with her father. In fact, what she discovers in accepting her fate is a measure of humanity. There is something honest and direct in the society of lepers here, living in a shadow world outside the city. But Cresseid has never been independent from circumstance. The community of lepers and their begging and their small comforts are really objectifications of what she has always faced. Cresseid, after all, has always depended on the kindness of strangers.

It is in the image of "passing," of the irreversibility of time, in the person of the father of time that the focus of the narration now moves from the superhuman to the human realm. The transformation takes place in front of our eyes, indeed, has taken place already as Cresseid picks up the mirror and sees the corruption of the flesh, an image for which, as a pagan, she has no real context.[8] It happens suddenly, a dream within a vision, in the form of this static debate, this masquelike encounter. In the driving history and temporal manipulations of Chaucer's *Troilus* the hope of redemption was, perhaps falsely, held out to us. In the *Testament* the static quality of the setting enforces its finality. All we can hope for is acceptance.

It is a significant part of the narrator's role in the *Testament* that he does not provide a means of perception and correction as does the narrator in Chaucer's *Troilus*. Rather, his comments resemble those of a chorus in Greek tragedy. The intercession here is perfectly in keeping with our own response at this point in the story:

> O cruell Saturne, fraward and angrie,
> Hard is thy dome and to malitious!
> On fair Cresseid quhy hes thow na mercie,
> Quhilk was sa sweit, gentill and amorous?
> Withdraw thy sentence and be gracious—
> As thow was neuer; so schawis through thy deid,
> Ane wraikfull sentence geuin on fair Cresseid.
>
> (323-329)

As a plea to Saturn, however, this passage verges on the absurd. Not the least of its weaknesses is that the argument would never convince Saturn, if the arguments of narrators can be said to convince characters at all. It is the sort of plea that might properly be addressed to Venus, who is, after all, part of the problem— she has participated in this "malitious dome" and is about to deliver the next part of the sentence. The timing of the passage is curious and does not seem to be accidental. It serves for the most part to vent our own feelings, to give air to a human resentment at the arrogance of the gods. Yet if anything, the stanza serves to irritate that arrogance and, in its doleful last two lines, emphasize the finality of Cresseid's fate.

Interestingly, Saturn has condemned Cresseid to isolation. He mentions the disease, but his statement emphasizes changes in Cresseid's social and moral qualities. The physical description of Venus' curse, which sounds so much like a pathology report that it has engendered medical studies, is more terrifying than Saturn's judgment, for it spells out exactly what will happen in ways we can understand. Even as the narration turns to Venus, we can expect the worst, based on the description of her in the parliament. We have been told of her venomous tongue, her eyes, one laughing and the other weeping, and the one concrete image in her portrait, a serpent. Venus at times resembles Fortune. But one could in fact find any number of allegorical females who are made to suggest qualities of impermanence, change, and fickleness—that which Cresseid has traditionally been vilified for. Cresseid's blasphemy is finally her lack of faith. When she later sends her soul on its way, it is to Cynthia, the goddess of the changing moon. Cresseid's symptoms are the signs of Cynthia, ironically a goddess of chastity; she wears on her face the pallor and black spots that Cynthia bears on hers. Cresseid wears the signs of the moon, suggesting instability. The narrator's own wish to change the mind of the gods is a desire to escape or ignore the very circumstances to which Cresseid is condemned, but which she has also caused.

The narrator's outcry here verges on being a contribution to the court of the gods. His rhetoric is more impassioned, more human in fact. He lets himself go, though at an oddly chosen time. One of the most characteristic apects of the various gods in their deliberations is a certain caution about what they will say. They are using rhetoric to convince. Their control is in fact mentioned several times, as in the doubleness of Venus and in Phebus' sweet rhetoric. But the narrator here takes no care to measure his effect. He merely says what he feels. Later Cresseid too offers measured cadences to express her pathetic state, but there the rhetoric seems to suggest a kind of ambivalence. Certainly, it says, Cresseid is not guiltless, but she has already been punished. She should not be punished this harshly. It is a justice without mercy. In any case, the narrator's interruption has a curious effect. It serves to push forward the judgment and to strengthen the bulwarks of the moral system that the plot embodies. He does not question that system so much as he asks that an exception be made. His emphasis on her former beauty embodies a failure of value as well as of logic. Her own reliance on her fairness is what got her here in the first place. In the end she gains humility, but in a world in which humility must be its own reward. Cresseid's gods ask for humility, but they do not seem to deserve it. Even the minor rebellion of the narrator here affirms that. But he rebels with a sigh, offering no hope to us, to his heroine, or to himself.

In a poem this short it is surprising to find so many transitional passages. The number of transitions testifies to the poem's intense compression and also indicates the number of times the plot switches scenes. We go from the narrator's study to the room of Cresseid to the parliament of the gods in her dream to the study, again to the dining hall, back again, then to the leper colony and that street scene where Troilus passes:

> That samin tyme, of Troy the garnisoun,
> Quhilk had to chiftane worthie Troylus,
> Throw ieopardie of weir had strikken doun
> Knichtis of Grece in number meruellous;
> With greit tryumphe and laude victorious
> Agane to Troy richt royallie thay raid
> The way quhair Cresseid with the lipper baid.
>
> (484-490)

This stanza also suggests the curious scale of Henryson's *Testament*. Dressed in alliteration perhaps it would not be out of place in epic. It has the elegance we might expect in romance and, were it not for the last line, contains nothing that might not be found in, for example, a Scots retelling of some French courtly romance. It does not remind us of most chivalric romances, nor even of Chaucer's *Troilus*, so much as of *The Knight's Tale*. This is partly because Henryson's hero remains undeveloped, and his function is closer to that of the stereotypical heroes of *The Knight's Tale* than to the rider of Chaucer's *Troilus*, who has already been introduced to us as the wretched lover of Book I and whom we can recall riding beneath Criseyde's window. But in the *Testament* the emphasis is on the ironies of fate. Troilus has indeed prevailed against the Greeks in battle, a fact that must temporarily call into question the treachery of Calchas and the relative wisdom of Cresseid, though of course Troilus will eventually die as Troy will fall. But there is nothing of this history in the passage. The battle is made to seem a part of the ineluctable system of ironies that damned Cresseid to her fate and that engineers the coincidence we will soon see. The emphasis is on coincidence and simultaneous narration—"that samin tyme"—which suggests to us that however poignant Cresseid's situation might be, it is not the most important thing in the world. The driving force is not history but the "ieopardie of weir," a wonderful phrase. Cresseid and the lepers seem to be in a no-man's land that has now been won again. The irony is that having left the Trojans for the Greeks, Cresseid will die on what may well be Trojan territory. The real problem, however, and the importance of this stanza, which incorporates the most carefully articulated and subordinated movement, is the last line again, which strikes us with the anticipatory fear of that meeting. Again we are set up for a scene that could wring out the utmost pathos. Henryson again will restrain that pathos by the more subtle irony of the scene. It is a style that seems to depend on an audience's need for extreme sensation. It is an art that achieves its effects by sternly controlling that need. Again the grand rhetoric of the stanza that moves us into the confrontation is made to contrast with the location of space in the last line (from the battlefield to Troy to the lepers' area) that puts into perspective the rhetoric. Such a grand style projects a world that Cresseid was once part of. It is not that we are asked to deny the power and the world implied in that stanza, but we are forced to contemplate its relationship to the world of the lepers.

Actually, the scene in which Calchas calls on his daughter,

135

having been mysteriously and tenderly called there by an in-
nocent child who has been asked by Cresseid to fetch him, is
one of the few moments in the *Testament* where sentiment
threatens to overwhelm us:

> He luikit on hir vglye lipper face,
> The quhylk befor was quhite as lillie flour;
> Wringand his handis, oftymes said allace
> That he had leuit to se that wofull hour;
> For he knew weill that thair was no succour
> To hir seiknes, and that dowblit his pane;
> Thus was thair cair aneuch betuix thame twane.
>
> (372-378)

His punishment can be justified on the extraneous grounds that
Calchas is a less than honorable man and that his treachery has
preceded that of his daughter. But in our poem there is no
emphasis on this. He is presented as any father faced with the
monstrous torture of a deformed child. His sentiments towards
her here seem decent, and his recognition of the problem seems
less a matter of abdication of responsibility than what any me-
dieval father in his situation would do. His response is nearly
maternal. There is a note of irony in a seer wishing never to
have seen this hour. He wrings his hands, both at the shock of
the contrast with her former beauty and at the immediate rec-
ognition of an incurable disease. The understatement of the last
line is characteristic of the narrator, and here it works to splendid
effect. But the real defense of this passage is the degree to which
its potentially maudlin quality is controlled; pathos does not
surface in the poem again until Troilus passes her by. What
the passage does is humanize Cresseid. There is a way in which
she has paid for her sins, and the innocent child who brings the
father to his daughter brings him to a deformed creature, but
one who is now somehow made innocent again. The pathos of
the child's calling the father from his dinner ushers in this sense
of innocence, and recalls a similar child in *The Pardoner's Tale*,
who there announces the fact of death. Where the quality was
sinister there, here it is truly pathetic, and skirts bathos only

by its humanizing of the heroine. Then too the compression of the poem allows us little time to grieve, a reaction not entirely typical of fifteenth-century poetry. Indeed, the poem's compression seems a defense against the obsessive repetition that could trivialize the experience and therefore obscure its moral and existential import. The power of the poem, that is, depends not on the constant excitation of the audience's responses, but on the careful restraint of emotion. The steady rhetorical stance is on the one hand a way of steeling us, on the other, a way of keeping the experience meaningful. Finally, this humble family scene, which has a certain Old Testament power to it, introduces what will be for the rest of the poem the dominant style. The courtly rhetoric and diction of the first half of the poem set an elevated tone. Now the level of style tends more towards the humble, the coarse, the creatural; it draws its class bearing from lepers, beggars, and saints, not from princes and ladies. The poem will return to a certain magnificence, but it will do so only after this purification through humility.

The way in which the poem ends—"Beir in your mynd this sore conclusioun / Of fair Cresseid, as I haue said befoir. / Sen scho is deid I speik of hir no moir"—is similar to the way most of the crucial stanzas of the poem end, especially those dealing with deep emotion, as if the verse itself were swerving from the path of sentiment. The lines are more difficult than they seem at first. The meaning of the "sore conclusion" may refer to the abrupt ending, the moral, the plot itself, the life of Cresseid, or her moral farewell. The "scho is deid" recalls the abrupt ending of the *Book of the Duchess*, but even that narrator had the grace to escort us from the world of the dream. There is no similar explanation here. It stops the poem cold, in a way that the poem itself has abruptly shifted at times.

At some points the stanzas end with exclamations, but more often they are self-enclosed. The difficulty of the narrative in the fourteenth-century examples that we have looked at is that even when their rhetorical materials claim to be aimed at eliciting a specific response from the reader, they are actually being subsumed under a larger narrative pattern, and it is that larger

137

narrative pattern which effects the change in the reader's con-
sciousness. In the *Testament*, the mode of address is the stanza.
And in many stanzas there is a sense of finality. Each seeks a
state of repose and offers itself up to our contemplation, much
as a pictorial representation might do. Indeed, the profound
restraint that everywhere marks Henryson's style is a means
to control our response. This is perhaps why the visual images,
which promise to be so striking and which seem almost to
become one of those lengthy iconographical descriptions of al-
legorical poetry in the fifteenth century, finally end up as rel-
atively brief figures. The rhetorical mode of address also explains
the time structure of the work, which after all does not move
as we would expect a story to unfold. The movement of the
story is much too abrupt, and we apprehend it almost as a sign
rather than a narrative.

HENRYSON'S POEM is filled with images of time and references
to time. Yet its action is so compressed that it seems almost to
be static; so these temporal images rarely influence our per-
ception of the poem's movement—they remain leitmotifs. The
poem begins with a peculiarly northern version of the spring
opening—cold, bitter images that suggest both the tragic (in the
medieval sense) and moralistic character of what is to follow.
The narrator too is old and dry; the landscape is dreary. As I
have suggested above, the disease from which Cresseid suffers
reveals in a brief moment the effects time will have on us all.
Even the intention of the *Testament*, supplying another ending
to a story rather than the more usual reworking of the tale
itself, has an anticlimactic cast. It is an act of criticism as well
as of continuation. In the guise of reopening the case, it closes
it far more definitely. In Chaucer's *Troilus*, as we have seen,
part of the narrative impulse comes from our expectations and
our hopes, our immersion in the stream of the narrative. Here
everything speaks directly to us, as if appealing less to our
perception of an ongoing experience than to our memory of one
long since past.

Indeed, in ways too extensive to explore here, the poem's

very justification depends on memory. For one thing, we are asked to recall Chaucer's poem. Cresseid's own tragedy consists only partly of her deformation; it also consists, as with the inhabitants of Dante's *Inferno*, of the memory of what she was like before. Her final speech is not just a plea to remember her but a warning to all those who might follow her path. That is, the deformed visage of Cresseid and the collocation of corruption, toads, and jewels markedly resembles those figures of memory that Francis Yates has described, meant to impress our imagination with the permanent importance of all this. The splendid portraits of the planetary gods, who appear in the dream within Cresseid's room, dressed in their peculiar garments, also conform to the ways in which memory figures are supposed to have been reconstructed in the imagination of the student. More generally, memory exists both in time and as a way of recalling time and, interestingly, is here presented not temporally but spatially, at a point when for the heroine it can no longer serve its redemptive function. Even the use of the grotesque in the poem is a form of compression. It transforms the ravages of time into the ravages of physical reality, of space, of localized description. The entropy that lies behind the history of earthly cities, and which is symbolized so importantly in the fall of Troy, is expressed not in war and ruin, but in the face of a woman.

In most fifteenth-century poems the medieval sense of physical corruption is obsessively tied to traditional themes of death and decay. In some great works—in the brutal torture of the York Realist, in the scenes of the knights of Chaucer and of Malory fighting ankle deep in blood—the image of the body is subsumed to some larger cosmic context. In Henryson the grotesque style becomes a statement in itself. The poem concentrates mercilessly on bodily decay, building from small hints like the odd rheumatic discomfort of the narrator, the figure of Saturn, to the loss of the heroine's beauty. At the same time, the decay is described in a style that retains its metrical integrity and that maintains a mellifluous Latinate syntax. Even the poem's urbanity is bizarre. For all its medically accurate detail, the real

139

impact of Cresseid's decay is in a kind of aesthetic reversal: we see the descriptive portraiture of the courtly heroine dismantled before our eyes. Part of the fascination is a process of anti-form. But the leveling is not entirely aesthetic, for Cresseid's fall is expressed partly in class terms. The food, dress, and beauty of the courtly lady become the crumbs, rags, and ugliness not just of the diseased or sinful but of all those who might not have the advantage of the artificial preservation of aristocratic life. The only democracy is that of time.

Cresseid bears only a surface resemblance to those medieval ladies whose beauty has faded like the snows of yesteryear or those who suffer, like Griselde, or Constance, or Emare, by the action of providence for the purpose of a test. The certainty and mercilessness of Cresseid's fate—it happens abruptly, like much else in this poem—is without either a Christian sense of forgiveness or the celestial distance of Chaucer's *Troilus*. Henryson's gods, after all, derive their authority from the imitation of legal deliberation as much as from theological sanction. Hence the emphasis on proportion and decorum in the introduction is ironic. That is precisely the aspect of the poem that is unresolved in the reader's mind. As C. S. Lewis has shown, Chaucer transformed Boccaccio's Renaissance work into a medieval poem. So too has Henryson taken Chaucer's poem and put it into a moral context that resembles nothing so much as that of the Old Testament.[9] Cresseid's sufferings resemble Job's more than do Griselde's.

Cresseid's consciousness, like her beauty, is limited by time much as she denies that limit. Her acts of defiance end up having repercussions she must face. The gods, in their half-Olympian, half-dream-world state, seem to enter into time only through their effect on the world below. Their actions seem to have no effect on their own future. Indeed, their casualness and their vindictiveness are painful precisely because they have no way of imagining what existence might be in time. They pass over the wreck of Cresseid's life with the same splendid indifference that they might over any other day. In a sense, then, Cresseid's worry that someone might see her as a leper is unfounded. As terrible as its judgment is on Cresseid, so too is the apathy of the universe towards her fate, tempered only by Troilus' memory of her. The lepers, after all, ask her only to be resigned to her fate. She gains some consolation from her complaint, which is in a way heroic and self-justifying, by the very fact that she asks to be remembered rather than forgotten. In the act of including herself in time and memory, by an address to us through the text, she achieves a kind of victory over her state. Even so, her warning is finally limited. Her advice is not to eschew earthly love, but to choose it more carefully and to treat it with more respect. Prudence, while admirable, is not nearly enough in a Christian framework. This limitation is not merely thematic, for the sense of measure and proportion that is at the heart of the poem's art, is also called into question.

Part of Cresseid's dignity at the end is expressed in the style of her speech, which is elevated without excess. Grand language in this poem does not exactly correspond to ethical qualities, for the lepers, who having lost their pride, respect the laws of the lepers, are in a Christian context more admirable than the magnificently described gods. Even in the transitional passages we have analyzed above, we characteristically begin with a sentence in the grand style and end with a stunning image that brings us down to earth: the inscription on Cresseid's tombstone, Troilus riding into the area of the lepers, Cresseid as a woman held "in common." At the end we look down with pity upon the lepers and the heroine. There is potential for irony here: we are not morally superior to the lepers; the rhetoric of the gods might well be called into question.

The *Testament* is a poem concerned with limits, and as it proclaims the limits of its own language to explain experience, it also serves to limit our vision. For solutions to the dilemmas it raises, we must go beyond the poem. Although in a markedly different way, we find again medieval poetry, either in its rhetoric, its style, or its narrative engagement, announcing its own limits. To this problem, which finds its origins in Henryson's medieval, rather than what is thought to be his "Renaissance" imagination, we turn in the next chapter.

141

Epilogue

Medieval literary theory assumed a more or less fixed moral order, which it was the poet's duty to impress upon the reader. On this theoretical level those scholars who alert us to the cautionary, exemplary, or ideal intention of most medieval narratives are correct. But in the most sophisticated works of the late Middle Ages this enterprise becomes complicated. As Auerbach concludes in his famous chapter on Dante's *Inferno*: "the principle, rooted in the divine order, of the indestructability of the whole historical and individual man turns *against* that order, makes it subservient to its own purposes, and obscures it. The image of man eclipses the image of God."[1] Auerbach's suggestion that the narrative presentation of certain episodes may compromise their moral intent has never been much explored outside of Dante studies, and even there it has remained controversial. The previous chapters have argued that this tension between ideal intention and narrative representation is the most characteristic feature of late medieval secular fiction in England. I have stressed what I take to be the chief manifestation of this tension, an anxiety about communicating immutable truths in a secular narrative fiction, which by definition takes place in time and which reflects the contingency and confusion of earthly existence. As a result, the poet had to invent ways to exploit or obscure this contradiction. Narrative discontinuity, visionary moments, temporal juxtaposition and foreshadowings, spatial form—all techniques used by writers of many different epochs—in medieval literature acquire a special, almost epistemological, importance. The individual chapters of this study have demonstrated the various solutions to the crisis of late

142

medieval narrative in England. The earliest Middle English romances of the thirteenth century assume an uneasy sense of community with their audience, strikingly different from the arch and sophisticated voice of French courtly romance. These early English romances skirt certain paths of development and avoid certain questions that might radically challenge the values of the audience, sometimes at the expense of narrative progress or stylistic coherence. In the great narratives of the fourteenth century, however, such as *Sir Gawain and the Green Knight* or Chaucer's *Troilus and Criseyde*, the very experience of reading reveals the limits of our own perception and understanding. The limits of narrative, a matter of skill in earlier poems, here become a matter of meaning. The dialectical and challenging potential of the crisis of late medieval narrative is fulfilled in these texts, but only momentarily. In fifteenth-century works, the poet seems obsessed with buttressing the moral edifice of the narrative, either by elaborate amplification as in the case of Lydgate, or by a severe limitation of affect and identification as in the case of Henryson.

In the remaining pages I want to suggest the relation of my reading of these texts to some common topics of the criticism of medieval literature. As recently as twenty years ago it was still possible to complain, with some exaggeration, that the criticism of medieval literature was still in a "nineteenth-century phase" or that the New Criticism had largely bypassed the study of medieval poems.[2] Now, however, it would be a slightly lesser exaggeration to say that the issues that have always confronted sympathetic students of medieval literature—the independent world of the allegorical imagination, the relation of voice and text to reader, the confluence of oral and written modes of discourse, the overwhelming strictures of conventional design and rhetoric, the necessary justification of art itself—have become newly important to theorists and critics of many different periods. If I have especially emphasized the role of the reader in the preceding essays, it is because the texts themselves, rather than the canons of modern criticism, demand such an

143

emphasis.[3] That is, the meaning of the great Middle English secular narratives is to be sought not in their "moral" or conclusion, but in the very experience of reading. It is generally agreed by most critics that the narrator, or the "persona," of most medieval poems is on some level a poetic fiction. It is less generally acknowledged that the reader in the medieval text is also dramatized. Apparently literal references within the text to audience or locutors are frequently invoked in what turn out to be ambiguous or ironic contexts and themselves should be interpreted with the same care as poetic images, which in fact they are. Such images are part of a complex code within the work that suggests and limits the possible range of our responses. We are, in a sense, the poet's most complicated characters.

The problem with discussing the question of the reader in all but the most recent literatures is that one is discussing not a single question but a series of questions, some of which require substantially different methods to answer and some of whose answers are especially difficult to verify. The distinction between a "modern" reading and a "historical" reading that purports to describe the response of the original audience probably raises more questions than it answers. Even if we had more information about the fourteenth-century literary public, this audience, as Dieter Mehl suggests, would remain for us a scholarly fiction.[4] Robert Payne has similarly reminded us that even if we could interview a member of Chaucer's audience we would have no guarantee that his or her response would be more valid than ours for any but linguistic information.[5] Neither Mehl nor Payne is denying the importance of recovering lost modes of understanding; indeed, both have contributed to that recovery. A case could also be made that our twentieth-century ironic Chaucer more clearly resembles a fourteenth-century Chaucer than does the fifteenth-century Chaucer that we often refer to when we speak of a "contemporary" response.[6] More generally, as Donald Howard has argued in *The Idea of the Canterbury Tales*:

you cannot speak of style without speaking of the effect of that style on the reader or audience. This means being subjective enough to follow one's responses and intuitions unabashedly, being (in Leo Spitzer's phrase) "mentalistic.". . . This has meant breaking down the traditional barrier between subject and object. . . .[7]

Because writing is a solitary occupation during which the audience can only be imagined or supposed, it makes more sense to say that a writer writes for an imagined or supposed audience. We can often grasp something about this interiorized audience from the work itself—it isn't mere shorthand to talk about the reader "in" the work.[8]

Although I have tried to distinguish above between a historically determinate actual audience, which I mean when I use the word *audience*, and the more complex "reader 'in' the work," which I mean when I use the word *reader*, my distinction is largely heuristic. As Walter Ong has argued in an important essay, "The Writer's Audience is Always a Fiction."[9] In fact, since the verifiability of the audience, let alone its response, is so difficult, the description of the reader is ironically more empirically responsible. Moreover, as the previous chapters have tried to demonstrate, even in medieval texts much more modest in their aims than Dante's, Langland's, or Chaucer's, the very enterprise of, and ambivalence towards, the creation of poetic images forces the poet to speak in a complex or double voice, only partly explained by the mode of original presentation.

Such a double voice is partly what complicates any application of traditional stylistics to Middle English literature. One of the reasons, for instance, that the methodology of Auerbach's *Mimesis*, which I described in my introduction, has been applied only fitfully to Middle English studies is that the close philological strategy of *Mimesis* does not always reveal what is central to many Middle English texts. Auerbach typically chose a passage at random and assumed that within that passage could be located the range of attitudes and modes of perception that inhabit the entire text. But one of the characteristics of Middle

English narrative style is an uncertainty and constant shift in tone that precludes such a microcosmic methodology. In addition, Auerbach's criticism, both in *Mimesis* and in the last pages of *Literary Language and its Public*, manifests a contradiction that I am not sure has been much discussed. He seems to be moving away from the intensely close investigations of his early work and moving in two paradoxical directions. On the one hand, both books depend on a rhetoric and an organization that seemed to validate, even to celebrate, a driving, progressive, Hegelian sense of history and literary history. On the other hand, the most startling perceptions in both works derive from a deeply personal, almost phenomenological understanding of how he, as a reader, was expected to react to the text. This second direction (which, as Howard points out in the remarks I have quoted above, also informs the best of Spitzer's work; but significantly, when Auerbach and Spitzer disagreed, it was on the ways in which the reader was being addressed, and it was Spitzer who returned to specific words as evidence) is only tangentially dependent on the trappings of historicism for which Auerbach is often celebrated.[10] In fact, Auerbach moved increasingly towards an almost subjective and inferential methodology, though not therefore historically invalid. Interestingly, some of his most assured analyses of medieval texts in *Mimesis*, such as those on the mystery plays and on medieval romance, rest on arguable sociological analyses. The previous chapters have taken this contradiction as a starting point and have tried to locate those moments in the text that force us to inferential and subjective response.[11] I have tried, that is, to redeem a critical embarrassment as a critical metaphor.

Since Dante deals with the question of the reader on a theoretical level, both within the *Commedia*, as if in commentary upon it, and in some of his other works as well, some recent criticism has focused on the place of the reader in Dante's text.[12] It is not quite as easy to trace such concern before him. Of course, medieval rhetoric in general was concerned with affect and response, but the theoretical level of rhetorical texts was not often high, and the best modern elucidations, such as Payne's book on Chaucer, deduce an aesthetic behind the handbooks and apply that to the author in question. The background texts, that is, require as much interpretation as the primary text. The crucial difference is that Dante's conception of poetry and of the role of the poet was unprecedented, if not in its specifics, then certainly in the grandeur of his aims. In inventing a new role for the poet, Dante had to invent also a new role for the reader. On a lesser plane this is also true of Chaucer, who defines the role of the poet and the uses of poetry in ways often ironically opposite to Dante's, as if in retreat from the magnificence of that calling. Because of this "invention" of the reader, neither poet is satisfactorily explained, even in terms of the narrator, by positivist descriptions of their audiences or comments by contemporaries about their work—evidence that often seems to disallow all but the most categorical response. But even in lesser and more "determined" texts, the most interesting moments of the narrative contain within them a defense of poetry, and it is those moments that the previous chapters have tried to describe.

Dante's moral vision is in fact inseparable from his redemptive, well-nigh messianic conception of the role of the poet, a conception that is no doubt as deeply implicated in his political hopes. Such freight is heavy enough for his own poem to bear, and it is arguable whether his synthesis is sustainable; his concern with correct reading and writing is an obsession, common to nearly all prophetic and apocalyptic poems. Moreover, Dante's intent is not only with the ethical behavior but with the ultimate fate of the reader's soul. By such a standard secular fiction is almost by its nature relegated to a lesser, fallen status. I have tried to argue that the uniqueness of Chaucer's *Troilus* derives at least in part from struggling with that status, struggling against it, as it were, and that it succeeds in its efforts by asserting its own negativity. A similar strain is noticeable, although less successfully negotiated, in most of the other narratives I have examined here. That is, the moral urgency of medieval poetic does not always, in fact only rarely, operates as a unifying force on late medieval secular fiction. More often the "inorganic" and "disunified" aesthetic form that modern critics have noted derives at least in part from an anxious tendency to circle around the almost overwhelming idea of a moral narrative, an ideal that probably could only be met by Scripture. If the dialectical challenge of the ideal Christian text eluded most poets, this is not to say that they did not feel some responsibility towards their readers. Even fabliaux could be justified as refreshment and recreation.[13] As I argued in chapter 1, the addresses of romancers as different as Chrétien and the poets of *Horn* and *Havelok* were meant to engage the reader in something more than entertainment, to educate the courtly reader in Chrétien's case, to include the reader as part of a larger community in the case of *Havelok*. But that intent, spoken or unspoken, was often at odds with the movement of the plot or the development of complexity in the characters. The most characteristic moments of these texts are often those in which the poet seeks to accommodate recalcitrant narrative images to his intent, and the most powerful moments occur when he loses, or gives up.

Many of the uncertainties that bedevil the effort at a historical description of the response of the medieval reader are uncertainties about the modern, rather than the medieval, reader.[14] I would question whether the experience of medieval literature is all that foreign to us. Rather, what makes us sensitive to the encyclopedic, quantitative, and "inorganic" form of medieval narrative is not the profound difference of such forms from those of modern—or modernist—literature, but the similarities. At least partly as a polemical device, some critics have been positing a fictional "twentieth-century" reader. (I confess to something similar in what is an obviously polemical description of the limits of narrative in my introduction. If the realistic, organic, continuously fictionalized novelistic world ever existed, it existed as a fiction and would demand not a natural but quite unnatural response from the reader.) Indeed, the process of reading that I have described in the previous chapters will be recognized as analogous in some respects to the notion of "defamiliarization" developed by the Russian Formalists and argued by them to be typical of much good literature regardless of period. I did not set out to describe such a process of defamiliarization; it seemed instead to proceed logically from the necessities of certain conflicts between a profoundly moral view of literature and powerful demands of narrative form.

Such a conflict is only partly explained by the clash of traditional morality and new artistic freedom. Rather, I would argue that the conflict has been implicit within medieval traditions and has only been brought to a crisis by manifestation in secular narratives. Within earlier medieval traditions of historiography and sacred narrative there were available methods of representation that could on the one hand adequately suggest the vagaries of human experience (as in, say, hagiography or chronicles) and on the other, identify the abstract pattern upon which the message of eternity is written (as in, say, biblical paraphrase or encyclopedic histories). But secular narrative, particularly when that narrative purports to include a version or metaphor for human history, as do most of the narratives I have examined here, forces a conflict between modes of perception that had previously been kept discreet or adequately subordinated. More directly than the notion of transition from symbolic to representational art forms, or from oral to written culture, such a conflict informs the peculiar shifts in scale that, in many Middle English narratives, dislocate traditional arrangements, relations, and harmonies.

We are used to thinking of a private, contemplative reader, holding his book like an object and, like a connoisseur, savoring the subtle distinctions of style. At the opposite pole, we imagine an audience listening to a speaker or singer, reacting to voice and presence, following the line of the narrative, and becoming themselves part of the performance. But the earliest Middle English texts already blur this distinction, and written texts in any case often adopt a tone apparently unique to oral presentation, drawing attention to themselves as performances, as compositions, and not infrequently the appeal of their art to us is in their self-consciousness, the way in which they make us aware of their own making. In the history of narrative since the Middle Ages such an element of self-consciousness has not been lacking, but it exists in tension with the conception of the work as an independently existing organism and serves primarily to underline the artist's creative struggle. Some would say that the process is now reversing itself, either as an ultimate extension of the romantic conception of the artist as hero or as harbinger of another revolution in medium, and that the act of writing has again become the subject of writing. I would not be the first critic to point out that some medieval and some post-modernist texts resemble each other in achieving their impact by a radical self-reflexiveness and self-consciousness, though both the intent and affect of that self-reflexiveness differ markedly.

The self-reflexive quality of medieval narrative can be understood in terms of medieval rhetorical theory. What the often detachable and discreet patterning of medieval rhetoric tends to produce is not a smooth fictional and narrative coherence, but the admiration, contemplation, or consideration of a set-piece. Even the most admired sentence patterns and decorative devices close inward upon a local unit and do not do much to move forward. When we are asked to savor or admire some minor description or scene, our admiration is meant to be directed as much towards the medium as to its object. Although Lessing argued that in poetry, unlike in painting, invention was more important than execution, medieval rhetorical tracts certainly seem to stress execution more. The literary picture, *descriptio*, *effictio*, ecphrastic rhetoric in general, is frequently refined or developed to the detriment of narrative progress. There was also, as de Bruyne has reminded us, a continuing debate in the Middle Ages about the same issue that Lessing addressed, *ut pictura poesis*.[15] The result was an overwhelmingly spatial apprehension of reality. Style was appreciated for its pictorial power on the one hand, and on its ability to communicate timeless, abstract truths on the other. In all cases the result is a passage or an entire work that seeks its validity not as a self-enclosed coherent form, but as an address, a sign, a communication to its audience or reader. Of course, all writing asks of us a divided response, between attention to image, context, expectation, and memory of what has come before. It is just that many medieval narratives leave the scars of that struggle on the face of their art.

Moreover, the rhetorical quality of medieval narrative fosters a consciousness of an addressed public, both in the writer and in his reader, as well as more obviously in an audience to whom a work is being read. There is, in general, a disputatious tone, which gives the style of some poets an academic or forensic coloring. Behind this tone lies both an implicit metaphor and a reminder of the origins of rhetoric in legal debate. The poet becomes, like the classical orator, a pleader. The audience becomes a jury. And his client, along with the major characters, is the plot or story he has to work with, and which he must put forth in its best light, twisting it here and there, interpreting its motivations in terms of the audience's values rather than the values implicit in the plot, even when there is a conflict between the two, perhaps even excusing the story by reason of its upbringing and previous associations. (That we are asked to judge is of considerable importance in light of our relation to certain characters. Gawain is, after all, on trial; Chaucer's narrator "defends" Criseyde; Henryson's heroine literally undergoes a trial in which our observance of the proceedings uncomfortably resembles her less-then-merciful litigators.)

The academic quality that I referred to is also ironically implicated in the presentation of information in medieval narratives. Chaucer, for instance, is full of wonderful lore and scientific information, and this encyclopedic quality, notwithstanding the fact that some of it is communicated to us by speakers who do not inspire trust, must have been part of the enjoyment his contemporary readers felt, just as Mann, Joyce, Pynchon, and certain other modern novelists, for all their difficulty, are also noteworthy for the poetry of fact. But just the way Chaucer tells it to us, and the tone he takes up, gives us the feeling that it is being told to us again. Chaucer alludes constantly to our previous familiarity with it all. When he does instruct us from point A, it is usually in the guise of characters like Pandarus or the Eagle in *The House of Fame,* and it is this quality which contributes to their fatuous side. In the fifteenth century more than a few poets begin to sound like Chaucer's characters. Information is again presented to us as if for the first time. This speaks to an almost consciously fostered new simplicity and suggests less a lack of ease with the knowledge itself than a certain insecurity with the system of which it is a part. Similarly, the use of high rhetoric is often undercut in late fourteenth-century narrative and often highlighted in fifteenth-century texts. For the Middle English poet, such elaborate rhetoric was a way of finding a voice, a way of authenticating his literary language. Even more importantly, however, rhetoric was a form of ordering experience, and it is the possibility of such order that late fourteenth-century poets were so equivocal about—and what fifteenth-century poets were so desperate for.

It is often assumed that great works of art will reflect the philosophical systems of their day, but as Iser has pointed out, their relation to ideas might well be more complex. They may not contradict those systems, but they will frequently explore the implications and needs that those systems leave unaddressed.[16] In Chaucer, as well as in poets like Langland, a complement to the reigning ideological system can be located: How, then, shall we live? How do the facts of theological truth affect our own experience and the realities of the social world (as well as the artistic means we have to express those realities and that world)? It is to these questions that the *Canterbury Tales* are addressed, but it would not be farfetched to locate the same concerns in the narratives I have discussed in the previous chapters. It is for reasons such as these that the relation of the great fourteenth-century poets to nominalism and Ockhamism is so complex. In general the effect of larger intellectual movements on medieval literature tended to be cumulative rather than topical. But more importantly, their fictions "complement" the very structures that these movements questioned. In their poetic images we find the same kind of skepticism that they would no doubt condemn if we could ask them.[17]

Even the overwhelmingly eschatological sense of time that I

earlier described as central to the late medieval world view is qualified by the experience of these fictions. True, the sense of an ending that completes the sometimes fragmented and discontinuous forms of late medieval narrative is not a "literary" ending at all. It is the apocalyptic vision that sees beyond the fleeting glimpses of imagination and mutable images of phenomenal reality. What that sense makes us realize is that the "stage" or world created by the poem, like the earthly stage upon which we work out our plots, is not the center of attention at all. The fictional world is aware of itself as a diversion, which at its best might suggest that the satisfaction we seek lies beyond the realm of art. Of course, poetry can admit that only discreetly and at its own peril. Moreover, even this self-implicating and self-consuming quality is necessarily partial; the apocalyptic sense that lies behind the structure of medieval narrative does not entirely limit the interpretation of characters within that structure. The reader, ever so slightly, is tempted to view the characters as God views the progress of mortal men, just as even more slightly, the poetic creation recalls the Divine Creation. That is, we know the end, we know what will happen, thanks to our previous knowledge of plot or genre or the assistance of the narrator. But for that very reason, our attention is directed to the working out of the problem, the various motivations and explanations that are advanced or inferred. The characters are thus given a modicum of "freedom" to make certain choices, to move in certain directions. Of course, since readers rarely have the sympathetic objectivity of deities, and since there are many more things to do while waiting for the end, this lateral movement becomes more interesting.[18]

Most mid-century criticism of medieval literature has tried to correct an earlier condescension towards the moral and religious dimensions of that literature. As a contribution to the annotation of specific passages and as a description of certain developments in intellectual history, this correction has been useful, even if the result has been occasionally to bury the text beneath marginally useful citations or to regard the poem as an alien and only barely decipherable code. A more severe problem

153

has been the assumption of a unitary moral and ethical program to be sought in all medieval works. My effort here, then, has been revisionist, to stress the impossibility of the unity celebrated by some admirers of the medieval world view and to argue that the real complexity and significance of medieval narratives lie in the gap between meaning and image, in the tension between mimetic detail and mythic structure, in the effort of style to dance towards at times and to evade at other times the great central questions almost necessarily avoided by the text. The performance of such poetry justifies by its very energy its own partial and peripheral existence, and like the poor juggler who has nothing to give to Mary but his skill, achieves a certain sanctity if only by its sense of distance from the center.

Notes

NOTES TO INTRODUCTION

1. On "paradigms" and narrative expectation, see Frank Kermode, *The Sense of An Ending: Studies in the Theory of Fiction* (New York: Oxford Univ. Press, 1967).

2. Ian Watt, *The Rise of the Novel: Studies in Defoe, Richardson, and Fielding* (Berkeley: Univ. of California Press, 1957), p. 23. The important attempt by Robert Scholes and Robert Kellogg, *The Nature of Narrative* (New York: Oxford Univ. Press, 1966) to rescue the study of narrative from the hegemony of the novel is hampered for me by their subscription to questionable interpretations of medieval literary practice as if they were unquestioned. A good history of attempts to come to terms with the question of structure in medieval narrative is available in William W. Ryding, *Structure in Medieval Narrative* (The Hague: Mouton, 1971).

3. The bibliography on the medieval sense of time is of course considerable. For general background see R.L.P. Milburn, *Early Christian Interpretations of History* (London: A. & C. Black, 1954); and Frank H. Brabant, *Time and Eternity in Christian Thought* (London: Longmans, Green, 1937). See also Beryl Smalley, *Historians in the Middle Ages* (New York: Scribner, 1974); C. A. Patrides, ed., *Aspects of Time* (Manchester: Manchester Univ. Press, 1976), especially for bibliography; also, Patrides, *The Grand Design of God: The Literary Form of the Christian View of History* (London: Routledge, 1972). Important for a specifically late medieval and English context are William Brandt, *The Shape of Medieval History: Studies in Modes of Perception* (New Haven, Conn.: Yale Univ. Press, 1966); and Robert W. Hanning, *The Vision of History in Early Britain: From Gildas to Geoffrey of Monmouth* (New York: Columbia Univ. Press, 1966). On the literary images of the concept of time, see the various essays in

Morton Bloomfield, *Essays and Explorations: Studies in Ideas, Language, and Literature* (Cambridge, Mass.: Harvard Univ. Press, 1970), esp. "Chaucer's Sense of History," pp. 13-26 (rpt. from *Journal of English and Germanic Philology* 51 [1952]: 301-313), and "Episodic Motivation and Marvels in Epic and Romance," pp. 97-128. See also Bloomfield, *Piers Plowman as a Fourteenth Century Apocalypse* (New Brunswick, N.J.: Rutgers Univ. Press, 1962). On the relation of such literary images to the real world, see Donald R. Howard, *The Three Temptations: Medieval Man in Search of the World* (Princeton, N.J.: Princeton Univ. Press, 1966); Christian K. Zacher, *Curiosity and Pilgrimage: The Literature of Discovery in Fourteenth-Century England* (Baltimore: Johns Hopkins Univ. Press, 1976); and Richard Glasser, *Time in French Life and Thought*, trans. C. G. Pearson (Manchester: Manchester Univ. Press, 1972). On linearity in medieval historiography, see Theodore Mommsen, *Medieval and Renaissance Studies*, ed. Eugene Rice (Ithaca, N.Y.: Cornell Univ. Press, 1959), pp. 265-348. Questions about the apparent dominance of the Augustinian notion of history can be found in F. P. Pickering, *Augustinus oder Boethius?* (Berlin: Eric Schmidt, 1967), vol. 1. A good deal of important material on time and history as conceived in the twelfth century can be found in M. D. Chenu, *Nature, Man and Society in the Twelfth Century*, trans. Jerome Taylor (Chicago: Univ. of Chicago Press, 1968). An important study of later literary manifestations is Ricardo Quinones, *The Renaissance Discovery of Time* (Cambridge, Mass.: Harvard Univ. Press, 1972). Perhaps most influential have been works such as Georges Poulet, *Studies in Human Time*, trans. Elliot Coleman (Baltimore: Johns Hopkins Univ. Press, 1956); and Erich Auerbach, "Figura," in *Scenes from the Drama of European Literature* (New York: Meridian, 1959), pp. 11-76. On typology in general, see Jean Danielou, S.J., *From Shadows to Reality*, trans. Wulstan Hibberd (London: Burns and Oats, 1960). Some useful connections between sacred history and literature are available in V. A. Kolve, *The Play Called Corpus Christi* (Stanford: Stanford Univ. Press, 1966); and Sarah A. Weber, *Theology and Poetry in the Middle English Lyric* (Columbus, Ohio: Ohio State Univ. Press, 1969). On fourteenth-century English literature, see James Dean, "Time Past and Time Present in Chaucer's *Clerk's Tale* and Gower's *Confessio Amantis*," *ELH* 44 (1977): 401-418.

4. "Letters on Chivalry and Romance," *The Works of Richard Hurd, D. D. Lord Bishop of Rochester* (1811; New York: AMS, 1967), 4:

300-301. A common enough analogy, but the most extended exploration is a work of Chaucer criticism, Robert M. Jordan, *Chaucer and the Shape of Creation: The Aesthetic Possibilities of Inorganic Structure* (Cambridge, Mass.: Harvard Univ. Press, 1967). The analogy also informs such studies as D. W. Robertson, *A Preface to Chaucer* (Princeton, N.J.: Princeton Univ. Press, 1962); and Charles Muscatine, *Chaucer and the French Tradition: A Study in Style and Meaning* (Berkeley: Univ. of California Press, 1957); Derek Brewer, "Gothic Chaucer," in *Geoffrey Chaucer*, Writers and Their Background (London: Bell, 1974), pp. 1-32. For reservations about art-historical analogies, see Elizabeth Salter, "Medieval Poetry and the Visual Arts," *Essays and Studies* 22 (1969): 16-32.

5. I have used Gotthold Ephraim Lessing, *Laokoön*, ed. Dorothy Reich (London: Oxford Univ. Press, 1965).

6. Joseph Frank, "Spatial Form in Modern Literature," in *The Widening Gyre: Crisis and Mastery in Modern Literature* (New Brunswick, N.J.: Rutgers Univ. Press, 1963), pp. 1-62. In a recent defense of his theory, "Spatial Form: An Answer to Critics," *Critical Inquiry* 4 (1977): 237, Frank makes an analogy between spatial form and Auerbach's definition of *figura*. My own sense is that figural representation is more resolutely historical than spatial form. But Frank is convincing in his minimization of his disagreement with Kermode and in his reply to Kermode's criticism of the theory of spatial form in *The Sense of an Ending*, which is why I cite both within my argument here. See also Joseph Frank, "Spatial Form: Some Further Reflections," *Critical Inquiry* 5 (1978): 275-290; and Frank Kermode, "A Reply to Joseph Frank," *Critical Inquiry* 4 (1978): 579-588.

7. Eugene Vinaver, *The Rise of Romance* (Oxford: Clarendon, 1971), p. 121.

8. Bloomfield, "Authenticating Realism and the Realism of Chaucer," *Essays and Explorations*, p. 186. A few other examples of the application of either spatial form or Lessing's "limits" to OE or OF works are Alvin Lee, *The Guest-Hall of Eden* (New Haven, Conn.: Yale Univ. Press, 1970), p. 86; Alain Renoir, "*Judith* and the Limits of Poetry," *English Studies* 43 (1962): 145-155; Norris J. Lacy, "Spatial Form in Medieval Romance," *Yale French Studies* 51 (1974): 160-169. A similar consideration informs John Burrow, *A Reading of "Sir Gawain and the Green Knight"* (London: Routledge, 1965).

9. On generic distinction according to the "radical of presentation,"

157

see Northrop Frye, *Anatomy of Criticism: Four Essays* (Princeton, N.J.: Princeton Univ. Press, 1957), p. 246.

10. Vinaver, *The Rise of Romance*, p. 5.

11. Ernst Robert Curtius, *European Literature and the Latin Middle Ages*, trans. Willard Trask (New York: Pantheon, 1953), p. 201.

12. See Robert O. Payne, *The Key of Remembrance: A Study of Chaucer's Poetics* (New Haven, Conn.: Yale Univ. Press for the Univ. of Cincinnati Press, 1963); also, Payne, "Chaucer and the Art of Rhetoric," in *Companion to Chaucer Studies*, ed. Beryl Rowland, rev. ed. (New York: Oxford Univ. Press, 1979), pp. 38-57. For a listing of essential works, see James J. Murphy, *Medieval Rhetoric: A Select Bibliography*, Toronto Medieval Bibliography, 3 (Toronto: Univ. of Toronto Press, 1971); and Murphy, *Rhetoric in the Middle Ages* (Berkeley: Univ. of California Press, 1974).

13. Erich Auerbach, *Mimesis: The Representation of Reality in Western Literature*, trans. Willard Trask (Princeton, N.J.: Princeton Univ. Press, 1953).

14. Erich Auerbach, *Literary Language and Its Public in Late Latin Antiquity and in the Middle Ages*, trans. Ralph Mannheim (New York: Pantheon, 1965), p. 298.

15. Peter Dronke, *Poetic Individuality in the Middle Ages* (Oxford: Clarendon, 1970), pp. 193-194.

16. M. M. Bakhtin, "Forms of Time and of the Chronotope in the Novel," in *The Dialogic Imagination*, ed. Michael Holquist, trans. Caryl Emerson and Michael Holquist (Austin: Univ. of Texas Press, 1981), 84-258.

Notes to Chapter 1

1. The classic distinction is W. P. Ker, *Epic and Romance: Essays on Medieval Literature* (2nd ed., 1908; rpt. New York: Dover, 1957). See too Auerbach, *Mimesis*, pp. 123-142; Vinaver, *The Rise of Romance*, pp. 1-14; Bloomfield, "Episodic Motivation and Marvels in Epic and Romance," pp. 97-128; D. M. Hill, "Romance as Epic," *English Studies* 44 (1963): 95-107. For a judicious survey of scholarship, see Lillian Herlands Hornstein, "Middle English Romances," *Recent Middle English Scholarship and Criticism: Survey and Desiderata*, ed. J. Burke Severs (Pittsburgh: Duquesne Univ. Press, 1971), pp. 55-95. Recent studies such as Robert W. Hanning, *The Individual*

in *Twelfth-Century Romance* (New Haven, Conn.: Yale Univ. Press, 1977), suggest interesting distinctions within "romance" itself along the lines of the present chapter. A similar distinction between thirteenth- and twelfth-century romance in France is made in an important article by Per Nykrog, "Two Creators of Narrative Form in Twelfth-Century France: Gautier D'Arras—Chrétien de Troyes," *Speculum* 48 (1973): 258-276, though his distinction seems to be based primarily on aesthetic differences. An important attempt to categorize the romances by length is Dieter Mehl, *The Middle English Romances of the Thirteenth and Fourteenth Centuries* (London: Routledge, 1968).

2. W. P. Ker "Metrical Romances, 1200-1500, I," *The Cambridge History of English Literature*, ed. A. W. Ward and A. R. Waller (Cambridge: Cambridge Univ. Press, 1907-1908), p. 277.

3. On the social context of medieval lyrics, see Stephen G. Nichols, Jr., "The Medieval Lyric and Its Public," *Medievalia et Humanistica*, NS 3 (1972): 133-153.

4. Among the most important of recent researches is the attempt by Paul Strohm to deduce medieval generic definitions from terms in the texts themselves. See his "*Passioun, Lyf, Miracle, Legende*: Some Generic Terms in Middle English Hagiographical Narrative, I and II," *Chaucer Review* 10 (1975): 62-75, 154-171; "*Storie, Spelle, Geste, Romaunce, Tragedie*: Generic Distinctions in the Middle English Troy Narratives," *Speculum* 46 (1971): 348-359; and "Some Generic Distinctions in the *Canterbury Tales*," *Modern Philology* 68 (1971): 321-328. A summary of definitions is available in Mehl, *Middle English Romances*, pp. 13-22.

5. For the purpose of convenience, all line numbers from the romances in this chapter are to the edition by Walter H. French and Charles B. Hale, *Middle English Metrical Romances*, 2 vols. (1930; rpt. New York: Russell and Russell, 1964). Archaic letters have been modernized both here and in other Middle English extracts.

6. Auerbach, *Mimesis*, pp. 143-173.

7. Unfortunately for our analysis, the road back to Denmark is contained in a missing leaf. In addition, a copyist's error seems to have omitted the journey back to England.

8. On the relation of chronicle to romance, see the important comments by M. Dominica Legge, *Anglo-Norman Literature and its Background* (Oxford: Clarendon, 1963), pp. 139-175. My comments on the "ground of being" of medieval history draw upon Brandt, *The Shape of Medieval History*.

9. Perhaps such evasion is characteristic of medieval political theory in general. See John Peter, *Complaint and Satire in Early English Literature* (Oxford: Clarendon, 1956); and Arthur B. Ferguson, *The Articulate Citizen and the English Renaissance* (Durham, N.C.: Duke Univ. Press, 1965), pp. 1-131.

10. Ernst Kantorowicz, *The King's Two Bodies: A Study in Medieval Political Theology* (Princeton, N.J.: Princeton Univ. Press, 1958), prints a number of illustrations. His discussion informs this scene. On the political theme in *Havelok*, see Mehl, *Middle English Romances*, pp. 161-172; and David Staines, "*Havelok the Dane*: A Thirteenth-Century Handbook for Princes," *Speculum* 51 (1976): 602-623.

11. Auerbach, *Mimesis*, pp. 110-111.

12. For an interesting reading of *Havelok* in social terms and for a comparison with a French analogue, see John Halverson, "*Havelok the Dane* and Society," *Chaucer Review* 6 (1971): 142-151.

13. Mehl, *Middle English Romances*, p. 172.

14. See Robert W. Hanning, "*Havelok the Dane*: Structure, Symbols, Meaning," *Studies in Philology* 64 (1967): 586-605; and Judith Weiss, "Structure and Characterization in *Havelok the Dane*," *Speculum* 44 (1969): 247-257.

15. See G. R. Owst, *Literature and Pulpit in Medieval England* (Cambridge: Cambridge Univ. Press, 1933).

16. See W. H. Schofield, "The Story of Horn and Rimenhild," *PMLA* 18 (1903): 1-83. Mehl, *Middle English Romances*, pp. 48-56, compares *King Horn* to *Horn Childe*, a later narrative.

17. *King Horn* is described by W. H. French as a *lai*. Though the classification seems to me less than helpful, his *Essays on King Horn* (Ithaca, N.Y.: Cornell Univ. Press, 1940) contains much useful information as well as a text.

18. This is not to say that it could not be geographically accurate. See W. Oliver, "*King Horn* and Suddene," *PMLA* 46 (1931): 102-114.

19. Something of the same is noticed in an excellent article by Mary Hynes-Berry, "Cohesion in *King Horn* and *Sir Orfeo*," *Speculum* 50 (1975): 652-670. See also Susan Wittig, *Stylistic and Narrative Structures in the Middle English Romances* (Austin: Univ. of Texas Press, 1978).

20. Dorothy Everett, "A Characterization of the English Medieval Romances," *Essays on Middle English Literature*, ed. Patricia Kean (Oxford: Clarendon, 1955), p. 22.

160

21. On the social makeup of the audience of the romances, a difficult question to answer, see the important essay by Derek Pearsall, "The Development of Middle English Romance," *Mediaeval Studies* 27 (1965): 91-116; also Karl Brunner, "Middle English Metrical Romances and their Audience," *Studies in Medieval Literature in Honor of Albert Croll Baugh*, ed. MacEdward Leach (Philadelphia: Univ. of Pennsylvania Press, 1961), pp. 219-227.

22. See Vinaver, *The Rise of Romance*, pp. 15-32.

23. For these reasons I disagree with the reading of D. M. Hill, "An Interpretation of *King Horn*," *Anglia* 75 (1957): 157-172.

NOTES TO CHAPTER 2

1. On structure, see Donald R. Howard, "Structure and Symmetry in *Sir Gawain*," *Speculum* 39 (1964): 425-433; A Kent Hieatt, "*Sir Gawain*: Pentangle, *Luf-Lace*, Numerical Structure," *Papers on Literature and Language* 4 (1968): 339-359; Sylvan Barnet, "A Note on the Structure of *Sir Gawain and the Green Knight*," *Modern Language Notes* 71 (1956): 319. The following notes are not meant to be exhaustive. For a good summary of critical opinion on the poem see the seminal article by Morton Bloomfield, "*Sir Gawain and the Green Knight*: An Appraisal," *Essays and Explorations*, pp. 131-157; the article originally appeared in *PMLA* 76 (1961): 7-19. It is brought up to date by Donald R. Howard's paper, "*Sir Gawain and the Green Knight*," in *Recent Middle English Scholarship and Criticism*, ed. Severs, pp. 29-54.

2. Howard, *The Three Temptations*, pp. 243-244.

3. A. C. Spearing, *The Gawain-Poet: A Critical Study* (Cambridge: Cambridge Univ. Press, 1971), p. 236.

4. See Larry D. Benson, *Art and Tradition in "Sir Gawain and the Green Knight"* (New Brunswick, N.J.: Rutgers Univ. Press, 1965), pp. 151-158.

5. On the rhetorical art of the *Gawain*-poet, see Derek Pearsall, "Rhetorical 'Descriptio' in *Sir Gawain and the Green Knight*," *Modern Language Review* 50 (1955): 129-134; Benson, *Art and Tradition*, pp. 110-166.

6. See esp. Erwin Panofsky, *Gothic Architecture and Scholasticism* (1951; rpt. New York: Meridian, 1957).

7. Described most eloquently in J. Huizinga, *The Waning of the*

Middle Ages (Garden City, N.Y.: Doubleday Anchor, 1954). On both the anachronism and usefulness of chivalric ideals in the late Middle Ages, see Arthur B. Ferguson, *The Indian Summer of English Chivalry: Studies in the Decline and Transformation of Chivalric Idealism* (Durham, N.C.: Duke Univ. Press, 1960); also Bloomfield, "An Appraisal," p. 138.

8. For different interpretations, see Howard, *The Three Temptations;* Alan Markman, "The Meaning of *Sir Gawain and the Green Knight,"* *PMLA* 72 (1957): 574-586; George J. Engelhardt, "The Predicament of Gawain," *Modern Language Quarterly* 16 (1955): 218-225; Benson, *Art and Tradition,* pp. 207-248; Peter Christmas, "A Reading of *Sir Gawain and the Green Knight,"* *Neophilologus* 58 (1974): 238-247.

9. For the background of alliterative verse as it bears upon *Gawain,* see Benson, *Art and Tradition;* also Marie Borroff, *"Sir Gawain and the Green Knight": A Stylistic and Metrical Study* (New Haven, Conn.: Yale Univ. Press, 1962); Arlyn Diamond, *"Sir Gawain and the Green Knight*: An Alliterative Romance," *Philological Quarterly* 55 (1976): 10-29.

10. Line numbers are to the edition by J.R.R. Tolkien and E. V. Gordon, *"Sir Gawain and the Green Knight,"* 2nd ed., rev. Norman Davis (Oxford: Clarendon, 1967).

11. On the further resonances of this opening, see Alfred David, "Gawain and Aeneas," *English Studies* 49 (1968): 402-409. Some background material may also be found in Theodore Silverstein, *"Sir Gawain,* Dear Brutus, and Britain's Fortunate Founding: A Study in Comedy and Convention," *Modern Philology* 62 (1965): 189-206.

12. On the place of game and holiday in the poem, see Martin Stevens, "Laughter and Game in *Sir Gawain and the Green Knight,"* *Speculum* 47 (1972): 65-78; Howard, *The Three Temptations,* pp. 243-244; Robert G. Cook, "The Play Element in *Sir Gawain and the Green Knight,"* *Tulane Studies in English* 13 (1963): 5-31; and John Leyerle, "The Game and Play of Hero," in *Concepts of the Hero in the Middle Ages and the Renaissance,* ed. Norman T. Burns and Christopher J. Reagan (Albany: State Univ. of New York Press, 1975), pp. 49-82.

13. Benson, *Art and Tradition,* p. 108; see B. J. Whiting, "Gawain: His Reputation, His Courtesy and His Appearance in Chaucer's *Squire's Tale,"* *Mediaeval Studies* 9 (1947): 189-234.

14. I seem to have borrowed this phrase from Muscatine, *Chaucer and the French Tradition,* p. 15.

15. See, for instance, William Goldhurst, "The Green and the Gold:

The Major Theme of *Sir Gawain and the Green Knight*," *College English* 20 (1958): 61-65.

16. Although by no means does this seem to me to support an allegorical interpretation of the shield, especially since the poet tells us what he wants it to mean. See Richard H. Green, "Gawain's Shield and the Quest for Perfection," *ELH* 29 (1962): 121-139; R. W. Ackerman, "Gawain's Shield," *Anglia* 76 (1958): 254-265.

17. On time, see Bloomfield, "An Appraisal," pp. 154-157; Laila Gross, "Telescoping in Time in *Sir Gawain and the Green Knight*," *Orbis Litterarum* 24 (1969): 130-137; John Crane, "The Four Levels of Time in *Sir Gawain and the Green Knight*," *Annuale Mediævale* 10 (1969): 65-80; and Victor Y. Haines, "Morgan and the Missing Day in *Sir Gawain and the Green Knight*," *Mediaeval Studies* 33 (1971): 354-359, which suggests some of the same ironic tension between author and audience as noticed here.

18. See Huizinga, *Waning of the Middle Ages*, p. 284. On the importance of visual description and action in the poem, see George Kane, *Middle English Literature: A Critical Study of the Romances, The Religious Lyrics, Piers Plowman* (London: Methuen, 1951), pp. 73-76.

19. Especially Alain Renoir, "Descriptive Technique in *Sir Gawain and the Green Knight*," *Orbis Litterarum* 13 (1958): 126-132. See also Benson, *Art and Tradition*, pp. 167-206. Borroff, "*Sir Gawain and the Green Knight*," pp. 91-129 has some brilliant comments on the conception of space in the poem. On the larger question of whether the poem is constructed on linear or spatial form, see Burrow, *A Reading of "Sir Gawain and the Green Knight*."

20. On the question of Morgan's role in the poem, see Albert B. Friedman, "Morgan Le Fay in *Sir Gawain and the Green Knight*," *Speculum* 35 (1960): 260-274; M. Angela Carson, "Morgain Le Fée as the Principle of Unity in *Gawain and the Green Knight*," *Modern Language Quarterly* 23 (1962): 3-16; also T. McAlindon, "Magic, Fate, and Providence in Medieval Narrative and *Sir Gawain and the Green Knight*," *Review of English Studies*, NS 16 (1965), pp. 121-139.

21. Charles Muscatine has described the *Pearl*-poet's style as a "defense" against a sense of "crisis" (*Poetry and Crisis in the Age of Chaucer* [Notre Dame, Ind.: Univ. Notre Dame Press, 1972]). He does, however, point out that compared to *Pearl*, *Sir Gawain* "gives greater

emphasis to the notions of disorder and of the imperfectness of human arrangements" (p. 68).

22. On the poet's audience, see Cecily Clark, "*Sir Gawain and the Green Knight*: Its Artistry and Its Audience," *Medium Aevum* 40 (1971): 10-20. On the social impact of the poem, see Morton Donner, "Tact as a Criterion of Reality in *Sir Gawain and the Green Knight*," *Papers on English Language and Literature* (1965), 1:306-315.

NOTES TO CHAPTER 3

1. On mutability as a theme in the poem, see Joseph J. Mogan, *Chaucer and the Theme of Mutability* (The Hague: Mouton, 1968).

2. *Troilus and Criseyde*, book 5, line 1809. Citations in my text are to F. N. Robinson, ed., *The Works of Geoffrey Chaucer*, 2nd ed. (Boston: Houghton-Mifflin, 1957).

3. On the question of unity and a "Gothic" aesthetic, see Jordan, *Chaucer and the Shape of Creation*. On the effect of narrative interruptions, see Bloomfield, "Distance and Predestination in *Troilus and Criseyde*," in his *Essays and Explorations*.

4. This is not to say that the poem is a philosophical allegory. See Theodore A. Stroud, "Boethius' Influence on Chaucer's *Troilus*," *Modern Philology* 49 (1951): 1-9; John P. McCall, "Five-Book Structure in Chaucer's *Troilus*," *Modern Language Quarterly* 23 (1962): 297-308.

5. Best exemplified by George L. Kittredge, *Chaucer and His Poetry* (Cambridge, Mass.: Harvard Univ. Press, 1915).

6. On the narrator, the seminal essays by E. T. Donaldson are collected in his *Speaking of Chaucer* (New York: Norton, 1970). A discussion of the considerable material generated by this topic can be found in Robert M. Jordan, "Chaucerian Narrative," in *Companion to Chaucer Studies*, pp. 95-116. A critique that suggests an approach that goes beyond the limitations imposed by concentrating on the "narrator" or "persona" is Donald R. Howard, "Chaucer the Man," *PMLA* 80 (1965): 337-343.

7. Generalizations about audience are complicated not only by the issues discussed in my epilogue but by the warnings in Robertson, *A Preface to Chaucer*, about the different forms of understanding a medieval audience might have had. See, however, Donald R. Howard, "Medieval Poems and Medieval Society," *Medievalia et Humanistica*,

NS 3 (1972), pp. 99-115, on this problem of historicism. Alfred David, *The Strumpet Muse: Art and Morals in Chaucer's Poetry* (Bloomington, Ind.: Indiana Univ. Press, 1976) describes the "pressures of orthodoxy" from the poet's audience. More specific studies of Chaucer's audience include Payne, *The Key of Remembrance*, esp. pp. 227-228; Alan T. Gaylord, "Chaucer's Tender Trap: The *Troilus* and the 'yonge fresshe folkes,' " *English Miscellany* 15 (1964): 24-45; Robert P. apRoberts, "The Boethian God and the Audience of the *Troilus*," *Journal of English and Germanic Philology* 69 (1970): 425-436; S. Francis Dolores Covella, "Audience as Determinant of Meaning in the *Troilus*," *Chaucer Review* 2 (1968): 235-245; Bertrand H. Bronson, "Chaucer's Art in Relation to His Audience," *Five Studies in Literature*, Univ. of California Publications in English, 8 (Berkeley: Univ. of California Press, 1940), pp. 1-53.

8. Bloomfield, "Distance," p. 211.

9. The question of the ending has been one of the most debated issues in the criticism of the poem, and it would be impossible to consider all interpretations here. See J.S.P. Tatlock, "The Epilog of Chaucer's *Troilus*," *Modern Philology* 18 (1921): 625-659; Donaldson, "The Ending of *Troilus*," pp. 84-101; D. W. Robertson, Jr., "Chaucerian Tragedy," *ELH* 19 (1952): 1-37; Howard, *The Three Temptations*, pp. 77-160; Alfred David, "The Hero of the *Troilus*," *Speculum* 37 (1962): 566-581; but see David's own partial retraction of his position in *The Strumpet Muse*, pp. 27-36. An important description of the traditions behind the poem is John M. Steadman, *Disembodied Laughter: Troilus and the Apotheosis Tradition* (Berkeley and Los Angeles: Univ. of California Press, 1972).

10. On the Trojan background of the poem, see John P. McCall, "The Trojan Scene in Chaucer's *Troilus*," *ELH* 29 (1962): 263-275; Bloomfield, "Distance"; Robert D. Mayo, "The Trojan Background of the *Troilus*," *ELH* 9 (1942): 245-256; H. M. Smyser, "The Domestic Background of *Troilus and Criseyde*," *Speculum* 31 (1956): 297-315. A different emphasis on the place and space of the poem is the fascinating article by Susan Schibanoff, "Prudence and Artificial Memory in Chaucer's *Troilus*," *ELH* 42 (1975): 507-517.

11. On Chaucer's settings in general, see Michael D. West, "Dramatic Time, Setting, and Motivation in Chaucer," *Chaucer Review* 2 (1965): 172-187; in the *Troilus*, see Sanford B. Meech, *Design in Chaucer's "Troilus"* (Syracuse, N.Y.: Syracuse Univ. Press, 1959), esp. notes.

12. I am borrowing the terms from Muscatine, *Chaucer and the French Tradition*. On this image see Alain Renoir, "Bayard and Troilus: Chaucerian Non-paradox in the Reader," *Orbis Litterarum* 36 (1981): 116-140.

13. See Bloomfield, "Distance," p. 215, n. 14.

14. Ralph Baldwin, *The Unity of the Canterbury Tales* (Copenhagen: Rosenkilde and Bagger, 1955).

15. Muscatine, *Chaucer and the French Tradition*, p. 140.

16. See Muscatine, *Chaucer and the French Tradition*, p. 60; Per Nykrog, *Les Fabliaux: Etude d'histoire littéraire et de stylistique médiévale* (Copenhagen: Munksgaard, 1957).

17. Jonathan Saville, *The Medieval Erotic Alba: Structure as Meaning* (New York: Columbia Univ. Press, 1972), p. 20. See also Robert E. Kaske, "The Aube in Chaucer's *Troilus*" in *Chaucer Criticism II: Troilus and Criseyde and the Minor Poems*, ed. Richard J. Schoeck and Jerome Taylor (Notre Dame, Ind.: Univ. of Notre Dame Press, 1961), pp. 167-179.

18. The phrase is David's, "The Hero of the *Troilus*," p. 580.

19. Donaldson, "The Ending of *Troilus*," p. 75.

20. On management of narrative time in the poem, see Bloomfield, "Distance"; Gerry Brenner, "Narrative Structure in Chaucer's *Troilus and Criseyde*," *Annuale Mediævale* 6 (1965): 5-18; Joseph Longo, "The Double Time Scheme in Book II of Chaucer's *Troilus and Criseyde*," *Modern Language Quarterly* 22 (1961): 37-40; Henry W. Sams, "The Dual Time-Scheme in Chaucer's *Troilus*," *Modern Language Notes* 56 (1941): 94-100; Benjamin Bessent, "The Puzzling Chronology of Chaucer's *Troilus*," *Studia Neuphilologica* 41 (1969): 99-111; and Wendy A. Bie, "Dramatic Chronology in *Troilus and Criseyde*," *English Language Notes* 14 (1976): 9-13.

21. C. S. Lewis, *The Allegory of Love: A Study in Medieval Tradition* (London: Oxford Univ. Press, 1936), pp. 195-196.

22. Stanley Fish, *Self-Consuming Artifacts: The Experience of Seventeenth-Century Literature* (Berkeley: Univ. of California Press, 1972), pp. 1-43.

23. G. T. Shepherd, "*Troilus and Criseyde*," in *Chaucer and Chaucerians: Critical Studies in Middle English Literature* (University, Ala.: Univ. of Alabama Press, 1966), pp. 85-87, suggests something similar. See also, Richard A. Lanham, "Opaque Style and Its Uses in *Troilus and Criseyde*," *Studies in Medieval Culture* 3 (1970): 169-176.

1. John Lydgate, *The Siege of Thebes*, ed. A. Erdmann and E. Ekwall, Early English Text Society, Extra Series 108, 125 (London: Early English Text Society, 1911, 1920). Citations in my text are to this edition.

2. The phrase of course is that of Harold Bloom, *The Anxiety of Influence: A Theory of Poetry* (New York: Oxford Univ. Press, 1973).

3. For a comparison of Lydgate's poem with the *Roman de Thebes* itself, see Alain Renoir, *The Poetry of John Lydgate* (Cambridge, Mass.: Harvard Univ. Press, 1967).

4. Renoir, *The Poetry of John Lydgate*, has a wonderful survey of critical reactions to Lydgate.

5. See, however, Anne Middleton, "The Idea of Public Poetry in the Reign of Richard II," *Speculum* 53 (1978): 94-114; also Arthur B. Ferguson, *The Articulate Citizen and the English Renaissance*.

6. In this, I am more in agreement with the argument of Derek Pearsall, *John Lydgate* (London: Routledge, 1970), than with either Renoir, *The Poetry of John Lydgate*, or Walter Schirmer, *John Lydgate: A Study in the Culture of the XVth Century*, trans. Ann Keep (Berkeley: Univ. of California Press, 1961). Pearsall's first few chapters are an important description of the literary climate of the fifteenth century.

7. There is much useful information on literacy and publication in H. S. Bennett, *Chaucer and the Fifteenth Century*, Oxford History of English Literature (Oxford: Clarendon, 1947).

8. Best described, of course, in Huizinga, *The Waning of the Middle Ages*.

9. R. W. Ayers, "Medieval History, Moral Purpose, and the Structure of Lydgate's *Siege of Thebes*," *PMLA* 72 (1958): 463-474. See the chapter by Pearsall on "The English Chaucerians" in *Chaucer and Chaucerians*, ed. Brewer, pp. 201-239. For further information, see A.S.G. Edwards, "A Lydgate Bibliography, 1928-1968," *Bulletin of Bibliography* 27 (1970): 95-98.

1. For a discussion of this context, see Denton Fox, "The Scottish Chaucerians," in *Chaucer and Chaucerians*, ed. Brewer, pp. 164-200; and Florence Ridley, "A Plea for the Middle Scots," *The Learned and*

the Lewed: Studies in Chaucer and Medieval Literature, Harvard English Studies, 5 (Cambridge, Mass.: Harvard Univ. Press, 1974), pp. 175-196.

2. When I wrote this I had not yet seen the excellent article by Larry Sklute, "Phoebus Descending: Rhetoric and Moral Vision in Henryson's *Testament of Cresseid,*" *ELH* 44 (1977): 189-204, which describes some of the ideas about fixity and order suggested here.

3. See Bennett, *Chaucer and the Fifteenth Century;* Huizinga, *Waning of the Middle Ages;* and Pearsall, *Old English and Middle English Poetry.*

4. As identified in the crucial essay by A. C. Spearing, "Conciseness and *The Testament of Cresseid,*" *Criticism and Medieval Poetry,* 2nd ed. (New York: Barnes and Noble, 1972), pp. 157-192.

5. Information on the intellectual background of Scotland can be found in John MacQueen, *Robert Henryson: A Study of the Major Narrative Poems* (Oxford: Clarendon, 1967); and Janet M. Smith, *The French Background of Middle Scots Literature* (Edinburgh: Oliver and Boyd, 1934); and Marshall W. Stearns, *Robert Henryson* (1949; New York: AMS, 1966).

6. Citations in my text are to Denton Fox, ed., *The Poems of Robert Henryson* (Oxford: Clarendon, 1981).

7. The matters of justice and Christianity have dominated most discussions of the poem in the past few years. Some articles that debate this are Ralph Hanna III, "Cresseid's Dream and Henryson's *Testament,*" *Chaucer and Middle English Studies in Honor of Rossell Hope Robbins,* ed. Beryl Rowland (London: Allen and Unwin, 1974), pp. 288-297; John McNamara, "Divine Justice in Henryson's *Testament of Cresseid,*" *Studies in Scottish Literature* 11 (1973): 99-107; Lee Patterson, "Christian and Pagan in *The Testament of Cresseid,*" *Philological Quarterly* 52 (1973): 696-714; Dolores L. Noll, "*The Testament of Cresseid*: Are Christian Interpretations Valid?" *Studies in Scottish Literature* 9 (1971): 16-25; E. Duncan Aswell, "The Role of Fortune in *The Testament of Cresseid,*" *Philological Quarterly* 46 (1967): 471-487; and Douglas Duncan, "Henryson's *Testament of Cresseid,*" *Essays in Criticism* 11 (1961): 128-135. Still important is E.M.W. Tillyard, *Five Poems: 1470-1870* (London: Chatto and Windus, 1948), pp. 5-29.

8. See McNamara, "Divine Justice."

9. C. S. Lewis, "What Chaucer Really Did to *Il Filostrato,*" *Essays and Studies* 17 (1932): 56-75.

1. Auerbach, *Mimesis*, p. 202.

2. A. C. Spearing prefaced his *Criticism and Medieval Poetry* with such an observation, seconded by some reviewers. Spearing's book appeared at a time when a dissatisfaction with the tenets of the New Criticism was beginning to be felt. In retrospect, the importance of his book for the purpose of critical theory, aside from its fine readings, was as a test case for the limits of the New Criticism, for he found himself often returning to the methods of the historically and philologically informed description that the New Criticism originally defined itself against.

3. The fullest bibliography is in Susan Suleiman and Inge Crosman, eds., *The Reader in the Text: Essays on Audience and Interpretation* (Princeton, N.J.: Princeton Univ. Press, 1980). Robert DeMaria, "The Ideal Reader: A Critical Fiction," *PMLA* 93 (1978): 463-474, has full and helpful notes. The more specialized question of the psychological basis of response receives a full bibliography in David Bleich, Eugene Kintgen et al., "The Psychological Study of Language and Literature: A Selected and Annotated Bibliography," *Style* 12 (1978): 113-220. The "aesthetics of reception" propounded by H. R. Jauss and others is most usefully surveyed in Jauss' own work, particularly *Literaturgeschichte als Provokation*, 4th ed. (Frankfurt: Suhrkamp, 1974), and *Alterität und Modernität der mittelalterlichen Literatur* (Munich: Fink, 1977). The most compelling "reader-oriented" studies of individual texts are by Stanley Fish: *Self-Consuming Artifacts;* and *Surprised by Sin: The Reader in Paradise Lost* (Berkeley: Univ. of California Press, 1972). See also Paul Alpers, *The Poetry of the Faerie Queene* (Princeton, N.J.: Princeton Univ. Press, 1967). Critics of reader-oriented criticism who point out that concern with the reader was already evident in Wayne Booth, *The Rhetoric of Fiction* (Chicago: Univ. of Chicago Press, 1961), are of course right. Such an approach is in a sense only the next logical step in the long line of Middle English studies spawned by Donaldson's work on the narrator.

4. Dieter Mehl, "The Audience of Chaucer's *Troilus and Criseyde*," in *Chaucer and Middle English Studies in Honor of Rossell Hope Robbins*, ed. Rowland, pp. 173-189. Mehl has also written a book on Chaucer, which, while it is meant as a general introduction, in fact contains some very important speculations about the creation of the audience "in" the *Canterbury Tales*. See Dieter Mehl, *Geoffrey Chau-*

169

cer: eine Einführung in seine erzählenden Dichtungen (Berlin: E. Schmidt, 1973). On this topic, see also Robert Kellogg, "Oral Narrative, Written Books," Genre 10 (1977): 655-665.

5. Robert O. Payne, "The Historical Criticism We Need," Chaucer at Albany, ed. Rossell Hope Robbins (New York: Burt Franklin, 1975), pp. 179-191.

6. See, for instance, the interesting observations by Alice Miskimin, The Renaissance Chaucer (New Haven, Conn.: Yale Univ. Press, 1975), p. 96: "We try to deduce the medieval audience chiefly by interpreting social history, by inference from symbols, and by imaginative projection . . . in short, by hypothesis and by abstraction."

7. Donald R. Howard, The Idea of the Canterbury Tales (Berkeley: Univ. of California Press, 1976), p. 18.

8. Howard, Idea of the Canterbury Tales, pp. 76-77.

9. Walter J. Ong, S.J., "The Writer's Audience is Always a Fiction," PMLA 90 (1975): 9-21. None of the critics I have quoted would discount historical evidence, but all suggest that we need to be careful about overly literal interpretations of the evidence we do have. See, for instance, Derek Pearsall's suggestion that the famous frontispiece to the Corpus Christi MS of the Troilus owes more to Chaucer's success at creating a fiction of oral presentation than it does to any actual conditions of presentation ("The Troilus Frontispiece and Chaucer's Audience," The Yearbook of English Studies 7 [1977]: 68-74). The same question had been raised by Derek Brewer, "Troilus and Criseyde," in The History of Literature in the English Language (London: Sphere, 1970), 1:195-228. Pearsall has provided a good summary of what we know about audiences, reception, and circumstances of production and presentation interspersed throughout Old English and Middle English Poetry, The Routledge History of English Poetry, 1 (London: Routledge, 1977). In any case, the impressive synthesis of information in Richard Green, Poets and Princepleasers: Literature and the English Court in the Late Middle Ages (Toronto: Univ. of Toronto Press, 1980), while it has the air of the devil's advocate about it, forces the initiative of proof upon those of us who ascribe to an older theory of an audience not exclusively composed of the court.

10. See Leo Spitzer, "The Addresses to the Reader in the 'Commedia,' " Italica 32 (1955): 143-165.

11. That such a procedure may not be limited to Middle English texts is evidenced by Robert W. Hanning, "The Audience as Co-Creators of the First Chivalric Romances," Yearbook of English Studies

11, no. 2 (1981), pp. 1-28. An excellent article by Evan Carton, "Complicity and Responsibility in Pandarus' Bed and Chaucer's Art," *PMLA* 94 (1979): 47-61, arrives at some of the same conclusions.

12. Robert Montgomery, *The Reader's Eye: Studies in Didactic Literary Theory from Dante to Tasso* (Berkeley: Univ. of California Press, 1979). See also Judson B. Allen, *The Ethical Poetic of the Later Middle Ages: A Decorum of Convenient Distinction* (Toronto: Univ. of Toronto Press, 1982).

13. See the important article by Glending Olson, "The Medieval Theory of Literature for Refreshment and Its Use in the Fabliau Tradition," *Studies in Philology* 71 (1974): 291-313.

14. See the useful analogies by Martin Stevens, "Chaucer and Modernism," in *Chaucer at Albany*, pp. 193-216.

15. Edgar de Bruyne, *Etudes d'esthétique médiévale*, 3 vols. (Brugge: De Tempel, 1946). See 1:230, 264, 278, 280; and 2:40, 72, 296. It is conceivable that another "spatializing" influence might have been the tradition of memory training inherited from antiquity. See Francis Yates, *The Art of Memory* (Chicago: Univ. of Chicago Press, 1966), p. 95; Howard, *The Idea of the Canterbury Tales*, pp. 134-209; and Beryl Rowland, "Bishop Bradwardine, the Artificial Memory, and the *House of Fame*," in *Chaucer at Albany*, pp. 41-62.

16. Wolfgang Iser, "The Reality of Fiction: A Functionalist Approach to Literature," *New Literary History* 7 (1975): 7-38. This article is now part of Iser's *The Act of Reading: A Theory of Aesthetic Response* (Baltimore: Johns Hopkins Univ. Press, 1978).

17. This is by no means to deny that these forms of questioning have some connection to the crisis of feudal development in the fourteenth century, a case made by Shiela Delany in "Undoing Substantial Connection: The Late Medieval Attack on Analogical Thought," *Mosaic* 5 (1972): 31-52; "Substructure and Superstructure: The Politics of Allegory in the Fourteenth Century," *Science and Society* 38 (1974): 257-280; and *Chaucer's House of Fame: The Poetics of Skeptical Fideism* (Chicago: Univ. of Chicago Press, 1972). The most thorough exploration of the philosophical implications of Chaucer's work can be found in Robert Burlin, *Chaucerian Fiction* (Princeton, N.J.: Princeton Univ. Press, 1977). On the epistemological dimension of *Piers Plowman*, see Mary Carruthers, *The Search for St. Truth: A Study of Meaning in Piers Plowman* (Evanston, Ill.: Northwestern Univ. Press, 1973). See also Russell Peck, "Public Dreams and Private Myths:

Perspective in Middle English Literature," *PMLA* 90 (1975): 461-468, for a more holistic version of the relation of medieval literature to culture.

18. Monica McAlpine, *The Genre of Troilus and Criseyde* (Ithaca, N.Y.: Cornell Univ. Press, 1978) makes a similar observation, p. 246.

Index

173

177

Library of Congress Cataloging in Publication Data
Ganim, John M., 1945-
Style and consciousness in
Middle English narrative.
Includes bibliographical references and index.
1. English poetry—Middle English,
1100-1500—History and criticism.
2. Narrative poetry, English—History and criticism.
3. Romances, English—History and criticism.
4. English language—Middle English,
1100-1500—Style. 5. Reader-response criticism.
6. Space and time in literature. I. Title.
PR317.N28G36   1983   821'.03'09   83-42559
ISBN 0-691-06580-2